Fusion \`fyű zhən\ n.:

the merging
of diverse,
distinct,
or separate
elements
into a
unified whole

Numbers

\ 'nəm bərz \ n.:

a theme throughout Scripture

by David Petersen

CONCORDIA PUBLISHING HOUSE • SAINT LOUIS

3558 S. Jefferson Ave., St. Louis, MO 63118-3968
1-800-325-3040 • www.cph.org

Written by David Petersen
Edited by Mark S. Sengele

This publication may be available in braille, in large print, or on cassette tape for the visually impaired. Please allow 8 to 12 weeks for delivery. Write to Lutheran Blind Mission, 7550 Watson Rd., St. Louis, MO 63119-4409; call toll-free 1-888-215-2455; or visit the Web site: www.blindmission.org.

Your comments and suggestions concerning the material are appreciated. Please write the Editor of Youth Materials, Concordia Publishing House, 3558 S. Jefferson Avenue, St. Louis, MO 63118–3968.

Manufactured in the United States of America

1 2 3 4 5 6 7 8 9 10 14 13 12 11 10 09 08 07 06 05

Table of Contents

INTRODUCTION

About the Fusion Series

Fusion—the merging of diverse, distinct, or separate elements into a unified whole. Fusion is a word that speaks of energy and excitement, whether you are talking about a style of music or a nuclear reaction.

God's Word is filled with fusion. The Old Testament bears many hints of events to come in the New Testament, yet we often miss the connection. The Gospel message of the Savior is seen time and time again in the Old Testament. Through this series you will come to connect—fuse—those events and messages for yourself and your participants.

Each study in the Fusion Series gathers stories from Scripture—both Old and New Testaments—around a common theme. Through the study of that theme, we pray that you come to a deeper understanding of the Gospel message of Jesus Christ as Lord and Savior.

Fusion—Numbers

This study will show how God uses numbers in the Bible, along with words, to reveal His love and plan for us in Jesus Christ. It will show how numbers play off of and build on one another to demonstrate God's design for creation and redemption.

What may not be clear at first is that the inspired authors of the Scriptures used not only words but also numbers to repeat and echo the theme of grace back and forth between the Old and the New Testaments. Numbers are always symbols. They are a way of speaking and writing meant to convey reality. They themselves are not the reality, but they represent or communicate what the reality is. God uses numbers and number symbolism in the Bible to convey the truth of His love. Some of that reality has to do with quantities, such as how high or wide

Noah's ark was, or how many loaves and fish were present. Often the quantities are meant to remind us of how God's grace intervened in the lives of His children in history. The ultimate reality God wants to show us is always who Jesus Christ is for us.

If this seems a bit strange, remember how Jesus explained the Old Testament to the disciples in Emmaus. Luke writes: "Beginning with Moses and all the Prophets, He [Jesus] interpreted to them in all the Scriptures the things concerning Himself" (Luke 24:27). Read also what Luther said about the Scriptures and their content:

> Thus all of Scripture, as already said, is pure Christ, God's and Mary's Son. Everything is focused on this Son, so that we might know Him distinctively and in that way see the Father and the Holy Spirit eternally as one God. To him who has the Son Scripture is an open book; and the stronger his faith in Christ becomes, the more brightly will the light of Scripture shine for him. (AE 15:342)

The Bible's purpose is to reveal God's love for us in Jesus Christ. This study will focus on numbers as a theme and springboard to study the Bible more closely, but its ultimate purpose is to talk about who Jesus is for us. It desires not only to show specific ways that numbers reveal God's plan for us in Jesus Christ, but also to help instill in the participants a desire to know Christ in all the Scriptures, for when He is known, the "Scripture is an open book."

Using These Materials

Fusion Series Bible studies are designed to challenge your participants to develop a deeper knowledge and understanding of Scripture. These studies work for either large-group presentation or small-group Bible study. While there are six sessions outlined in the book, there are no suggested time limits for each section of the lesson. The level of participant interest, discussion, and further questions will help establish the length of time to spend on each section. This flexibility also allows you to use this material for more than six one-hour sessions. You can easily adapt this material to twelve or more hour-long lessons.

Each session contains reproducible participant pages. These pages may be given to participants as you work through the lesson together in class. As an alternative, you may give copies of these pages to participants in advance of the session so that they may complete their personal study before coming to class.

The leader's materials work through the questions from the participant pages and provide additional commentary and insights for the Bible class leader. You will want to study these notes as you prepare to lead each session.

It is assumed that the Bible class leader will have the usual basic equipment and supplies available—pencils or pens for each participant and a chalkboard or its equivalent (white board, overhead transparency projector, or newsprint pad and easel) with corresponding markers or chalk. Encourage the participants to bring their own Bibles so that they can mark useful passages and make notes to guide their personal Bible study and reference. Do provide additional Bibles, however, for visitors or participants who do not bring one. The appropriate participant pages should be copied in a quantity sufficient for the class.

1

The Counting God

Lesson Focus

There are lots of numbers in the Bible. There are especially a lot of threes, sevens, tens, twelves, and forties. You can probably think of lots of things from Scripture that come in those numbers. It almost seems like nothing ever happens in the Bible that is not somehow related to one of those numbers. This lesson will begin to open up these numbers. We will begin to look for patterns and start to see how numbers communicate more than a mere amount. We will especially look for repetition and relationships between various events in the history of God's people.

We also want to consider numbers that describe strange things. The Bible records details like 144,000 saints in heaven and four six-winged, multi-faced creatures. Those quantities are very exact and we want to think about what they describe, how literal they are, and again, how they relate to other numbers in the Bible. Since every word of the Holy Scriptures is meant for our learning, and nothing has been written by accident or coincidence, these numbers have meaning. In beginning to unpack the meaning, this lesson will serve as a foundation for the lessons that follow.

Opening Prayer

Blessed Lord, since You have caused all Holy Scriptures to be written for our learning, grant that we may so hear them, read, mark, learn, and take them to heart that by patience and comfort of Your holy Word we may embrace and ever hold fast the blessed hope of everlasting life; through Jesus Christ, Your Son, our Lord, who lives and reigns with You and the Holy Spirit, one God, now and forever. Amen.

(Collect 165, *LW*, p.156)

God Counts and Biblical Numbers

What are some common numbers in the Bible? Are there any patterns?

Ask the students for numbers from the Bible. You might start with "How many days and nights did it rain when Noah went into the ark?" Then see if they can think of other numbers or groups of numbers in the Bible. Ask if they can think of other major repetitive numbers. Since you've asked about the flood, they'll probably get forty right away. Try to get a couple of examples also for three, seven, ten, and twelve. You might have to prompt them. If necessary, try asking questions like "How many commandments are there?" or "How many days was Jesus in the tomb?" Your goal is to get them to see how these numbers repeat and tie the story of creation and salvation together.

Here is a list of some of the major numbers and events in the Bible. You and your students will probably think of even more. We do not want to unpack these numbers just yet, but merely raise awareness of them. There are also other numbers this study will consider, such as two, four, five, seventy, and one thousand. The purpose here is merely to get the students to recognize there are patterns.

Forty: years that Israel wandered in the desert; days of our Lord's fasting and temptation; days and nights of rain at the time of Noah; days from Easter to the Ascension. (While not in the Bible, some students might also note that Lent is forty days long.)

Three: Trinity (Matthew 28 and baptismal formula); days until Jonah's deliverance from the great fish; the inner circle of the disciples (Peter, James, John); days Jesus was in the tomb. ("Three days" was a Jewish idiom meaning the day after tomorrow. Three days equaled part of Friday [1], all day Saturday [2], and part of Sunday [3], as opposed to three twenty-four-hour days equaling seventy-two hours.)

Seven: days in the week (creation); years of good harvest and then of famine in Egypt; number of churches in St. John's vision; number of gifts of the Spirit. (Again, while not in the Bible, some students may notice the Easter season is seven weeks long.)

Ten: Commandments; plagues in Egypt; lamp-bearing virgins in the parable; lepers seeking mercy.

Twelve: Jacob's sons; tribes of Israel; disciples; baskets of leftover bread and fish after the feeding of the five thousand; months (the Hebrew year had twelve months like our modern calendar).

Symbolism Based in History

Do numbers mean more than what they count? What do the numbers 1776 and 1492 mean to you? What about thirteen stripes and fifty stars on an American flag? How many shots in a twenty-one gun salute? What does it mean?

The United States Constitution was signed in the year 1776. Christopher Columbus sailed from Spain in 1492. The thirteen stripes on an American flag represent the thirteen original colonies and the fifty stars represent the current states. Because of those events or truths, those numbers are all important to Americans. Numbers can be literal, and yet at the same time speak to something more. A Fourth of July party might have a cake with fifty or thirteen candles. The number would be literal, but it would also be representative, symbolic of the United States.

A twenty-one gun salute is seven guns firing three times each in unison. It is a literal twenty-one shots, but it sounds like three. Most hearers can't tell the difference between a twenty-one gun salute (with seven guns firing) and an eighteen or a twenty-four gun salute (with six or eight guns firing). But we want a twenty-one gun salute. That is the right number. A twenty-one gun salute calls to mind a sense of fullness and completion. It signifies a full military honor.

Most of the numbers in the Bible are literal. They actually measure something. For instance, we believe that Jesus fasted for forty actual days in the desert. He might have been a bit short of nine-hundred-sixty hours (forty days times twenty-four hours). He might not have started the first day until 8:00 in the morning, or even 12:00 noon—it would still have counted as a day. Jesus might have eaten the evening of the fortieth day. Nonetheless, these were forty real days. That number helps tie Jesus' fast to the history of Israel. The number of days is not accidental. It is literal and symbolic. It is meant to remind us of Israel's wandering in the desert, the days and nights of rain that caused the flood, and so forth. It connects Jesus to His people. But even that is no coincidence. For it could have rained thirty-eight days and thirty-eight nights; the Israelites could have wandered for thirty-seven or forty-two years. Forty symbolizes fullness in creation. We will explore this more fully later in this study.

God Counts in Love

Read Genesis 1:1–2:3. How are the days counted? How does this relate to Sunday morning worship?

The Bible is full of counting. At the very beginning, God was already counting. The first thing He did was to create light and count the first day. It was very orderly and structured. It was a mathematical creation, one day upon another, so that two followed one and three followed two, and so forth. Each day added up to get to the total. Finally there were six days. God finished creation. When He reached the seventh day, He rested.

Ask the students if the days of the week have meaning in the life of Christ. Think particularly about Holy Week. They'll probably come up with Maundy Thursday, Good Friday, and Easter pretty quickly. You might want to remind them of the times Jesus healed on the Sabbath and how He rode into Jerusalem on a Sunday. They may not realize that Judas made his deal with Caiaphas on a Wednesday. Because of what happened on those days of the week, they are important to the Church.

In the Early Church, Christians fasted especially on Wednesdays and Fridays during Lent. They did this because those were the days of Jesus' betrayal and death. The Church Year revolves around Easter. Unlike Christmas, which is always on December 25 but can be any day of the week, Easter is always on a Sunday. The calendar day can change, but the weekday cannot. The Church associates Easter with the Jewish Passover because Jesus was crucified as the Passover lambs were being sacrificed in the temple (John 19:14). The problem is that, in Bible times, the Jewish Passover was the 14th of Nisan. It was like Christmas. It was tied to a calendar date. It fell on a different weekday every year. The year Jesus died, it fell on Friday, so three days later was Sunday. In figuring out how to celebrate Easter, Christians decided the day of the week took precedence over the calendar date of the Passover. They wanted Easter on Sunday. That is why today Easter is the Sunday that follows the "first full moon after the spring equinox." It always falls between March 25 and April 25 (*Lutheran Worship: History and Practice,* p. 171). It is complicated, but that seems to be the best way to get Easter on Sunday, Good Friday on Friday, Maundy Thursday on Thursday, and Palm Sunday on Sunday. It wouldn't have to be this way. But the Church has historically found meaning in the days of the week. Her wisdom suggests we contemplate certain events of our Lord's life on the day of the week that they happened.

The life of the Christian finds its ultimate meaning and source in the life of Jesus Christ. We worship on Sunday mornings as a weekly reminder of the resurrection of Jesus Christ. It is not merely that Jesus rose on a Sunday. It is that in rising He inaugurated our coming resurrection. We too will rise. We come to church on this day as a remembrance of how He bought and won us and as a sign of the victory to come. Understanding and counting these days of the week in the life of Christ helps to give meaning to our worship and to encourage us in our daily lives.

Read Matthew 10:28–31. What does this tell us about God?

God cares about details. He leaves nothing to chance. He counts the sparrows, but, more than that, every hair on your head counts to Him. God loves you more than sparrows!

Read again the familiar words of John 3:16. How does God love you? What does the word *so* mean in the phrase *God so loved the world*?

Our God does not love us the way that some people love cats or chocolate. It is not a generic or even a general love. His love is intimate, precise, and individually specific. It is fatherly love, custom-made for each child, accurately cut and fit to each personality. Every hair on your head counts to God. It counts to Him even more than it counts to you. He loves you more than anyone else does. He loves you more than you love yourself, more than you are even capable of loving yourself. He loves you right down to the very last hair.

That love has been shown to us in a very specific way. The word *so* in John 3:16 is an adverb. The word *so* is often used in English to modify a verb in degree. Thus *He was so tired* is meant to be more emphatic or to indicate a greater degree of tiredness than simply *He was tired.* This is the way that *so* might sound to us in John 3:16. It might sound as though it reads "God loved the world so much that He gave His only Son." But that is not the word behind *so* here. It is not an adverb modifying degree. In Greek it is the word *houtos.* It means "thus" or "in this way." This is the way we use the word *so* when we say "Say it isn't so!" or "Is that so?" John 3:16 could be translated very literally as "God loved the world this way: He gave His only Son." This is how God has loved us. He didn't sit in heaven and think nice things about us or scribble our names on His notebook only to hide it from His mother. He gave His only Son into death to win us. It is that same love—that did not love His own life—that loved us to the end—that causes Him to count the hairs on our heads.

There is another important little word in this verse. It is the English word *that.* Behind this word is the Greek word *hoste.* It means "so that" or "therefore." It is a bit like the word *because* in reverse. The word *because* requires the effect to be stated first. The cause comes after *because.* We say "I bought bread because I was hungry." We do not say "I was hungry because I bought bread." That would be backwards. The word *that* in John 3:16 is used in an archaic way to translate *hoste.* It means "such" or "so." In this way the cause comes first and the effect follows the word *that.* Whereas we would say "I bought bread because I was hungry," we would say "I was hungry so I bought bread" or we could say "Since I was hungry I bought bread." The word *hoste* works like the word *since.* The thing to notice in John 3:16 then is that the way God has loved us (giving His only Son into death for us) came about because God loved us. He loved us so He gave His Son or we might say "since He loved us He gave us His Son."

It is not as though the cross changed the way God feels about us. He has always loved us. It is not as though He hated us because we were sinners, but then He gave His Son to die for us and changed His mind because of it. He has always loved us! The giving of His Son, His suffering, death, and resurrection, do not make the Father love us. Rather they show us the Father's love. This is how God has loved us. He has not changed, but we have. He did not change His mind about us, He changed our minds about Him. He showed us His love by paying for our sins, by dying in our place, by loving us to the end. Now we are free to believe in Him and not perish but have everlasting life. He loves us more than sparrows and lilies, indeed.

Read Luke 15:4–7. How many sheep are there? How does the shepherd know?

The shepherd counts the sheep. There are supposed to be one hundred and each one is precious to him. There are only ninety-nine. One lost sheep is a mere one percent of his total flock, but it is valuable to him. He is willing to suffer whatever trouble and danger it takes to get that single sheep back. The other parables in Luke 15 echo this same idea. These include the parable of the lost coin (Luke 15:8–10) and the parable of the lost son (Luke 15:11–32). In all three parables, we see how God counts and keeps track of each soul. Again, the number of sheep, one hundred, and the number of coins, ten, are numbers of completion. We will deal with that concept more fully later in the study, but for now it is worth pointing out these numbers as common repetitions. Since these are parables, we do not expect that they had to be actual historical events. Thus we see the details, including the numbers, to often represent more than merely an amount.

Read Ezekiel 40–41. How many times does the word *cubit* occur? How about *rod*? What numbers are mentioned? What else? Why are the measurements so precise?

The measurements are precise because God cares about the details. He is precise in his dealings with man. This does not mean that God is a micro-manager, interfering with our lives and denying us freedom. Rather He is intimately and personally involved. He cares if you have a hangnail or a bad hair day. He cares if your boyfriend was rude or you feel dumpy for no real reason at all. Nothing about you is trivial to Him. Everything about you, and this world, matters to Him. He did not send His Son in vain. He sent Him in perfect love. He counts the hairs on your head and you are worth more than sparrows. We'll come back to this text later and consider what the numbers remind us of; for now let it be enough to show how precise God is in His dealings with men.

God Counts the Innumerable.

The Greek word for "numbered" or "counting" in Matthew's Gospel is the word behind our word *arithmetic.* We might say, "God does the math." He even does the math when it is impossibly hard.

Read Psalm 40. What is the number of God's merciful works? What makes David sing? Pay special attention to verses 11–13. How many evils surround David? Who can count them? What is the familiar phrase in this psalm?

Notice the counting. David cried out that his troubles were without number (12). These evils that surrounded him include his own sins. They were more than the hairs of his head. Yet the Lord was pleased to save him (12–13). What David asks for in verse 13, help and deliverance, is personified in the Messiah. The Messiah is the Helper and Deliverer. David points this out in verse 17b, for God Himself is the Messiah, "You are my help and my deliverer; do not delay, O my God!"

Some of the students may notice the echo in verse 13, "Be pleased, O LORD, to deliver me! O LORD, make haste to help me!" with the opening Versicles for Matins and Vespers. In Matins and Vespers, we pray: "Make haste, O God, to deliver me" and "Make haste to help me, O Lord." That prayer comes from the first verse of Psalm 70, another psalm of David, so the echo is not surprising. This is something David liked to pray. He was always praying for help and deliverance. He found it in His own descendent born one thousand years later to the Virgin Mary.

David has a new song to sing (40:3) because sins and trouble have been removed. Though they were beyond the reckoning power of men, innumerable for him (verse 12), they have been counted by God and countered with innumerable mercies and grace. In Christ they don't count! One time David's sins did count. So did ours. Every one of them counted when Jesus was scourged by Pilate's soldiers and was nailed to the cross. Every one of them counted when He hung in agony and sacrificed Himself. David's sins counted. So did ours. But now they are gone. They have all, every single one of them, David's and ours, been counted and forgiven by the Deliverer.

Sinners Count to Him.

Read Luke 7:37–39. Think to yourself about Jesus' words about counting the hairs of our heads while you read this. How does that color what the woman does to our Lord's feet with her hair? Now read Luke 7:44–50.

Every hair counted as it brushed across those dirty feet. Those feet would soon be pierced and bleed. The blood that came from them would wash this woman clean. Indeed, she loved much. But she did not love as much as the One who counted and loved those hairs. Every hair on her head counted! Every hair was felt and known. Every hair was honored and loved as it brushed across Jesus' feet. Jesus was more aware of her, of the hairs on her head, than she was. She went in peace that day because Jesus went to the cross, anointed by oil, tears, and hair to be her forgiving King, because she counted to Him even though she didn't count to the Pharisees. That is the peace that passes all understanding.

God cares about the details. He loves every hair on your head. He loves you more than you love yourself, more than you are capable of containing, so that David also writes "My cup overflows" (Psalm 23:5). God counts, but it seems as though He is a bad mathematician. It is not an exact punishment for each sin and no more. He pays for the sins of those who will not believe in Him (Pharaoh, Judas, Herod the Great, etc.) or receive the benefit of His love. He gives His life for the sins of whole world. We see this same over-generosity in the feeding of the five thousand (Matthew 14:20), in the feeding of His people in the wilderness (Exodus 16:16–18), and in the miracle at Cana. Here He gave more than the people could eat or drink. Jesus created the equivalent of between six hundred and nine hundred bottles of wine at Cana—more than could have been drunk in one night by a village (John 2:1–11). David rightly recognizes a pattern in God's giving mercy when He praises God and says, "My cup overflows." God always gives more than we can contain. The Good News of Jesus Christ is not equal in goodness to the badness of our rebellion or sins. It is, instead, so great that it is not worthy of comparison, like considering the height of a blade of grass to the height of the Empire State Building.

An Introduction to the Symbolism of Biblical Numbers

Read Revelation 7:4–9. How many saints does John see? Notice the number in verse 4 and the number in verse 9. What are some clues that this is a symbolic number and not literal? What are its factors? And what does this tell us about how many people will be in heaven?

One of the ways this counting God reveals Himself and His love for us is through numbers. It is not the only way. It is not even the chief way. But it is an important way. Besides showing us that God cares about the details, the numbers in the Bible also show us a pattern to God's care for us. The numbers in the Bible are usually, but not always, precise measurements of the physical reality. When they are not precise measurements of physical reality, they are symbols of divine counting and are not literal. We can tell this is a symbolic number because of its context. John sees this multitude in a vision. We don't understand all these seals and horses and things to be literal either. They all represent something else.

The 144,000 of verse 4 is not an exact count of the elect. In fact, we expect far more than that in heaven, more than any man can number (verse 9) but which God numbers. God counts them all. Men are capable of counting, adding, subtracting, and multiplying with the number 144,000 even if some of us need a calculator to do it. But in verse 9, John says that no one can number these people. Imagine how great that number is! Imagine all the thousands and thousands of believers, of God's people, from every tribe, nation, and people, from every age and time of the earth. The number 144,000 represents the great multitude, that is, the large number of saints who will be in heaven. Even more significantly, it represents the fullness of that group—the perfect totality of the elect. Not a single one will be missing. Everyone will be accounted for.

The symbolism of the number 144,000 comes from its factors. A factor is a smaller number that makes up a larger number by multiplication. Three is a factor of six because 3 X 2 = 6. 144,000 is made up of 2 X 2 X 2 X 2 X 2 X 2 X 2 X 3 X 3 X 5 X 5 X 5, but it makes more sense for biblical symbolism to break it up as 12 X 12 X 1000. Understanding the symbolism of biblical numbers often means not breaking them into the lowest possible factors, but into the factors that have meaning. In the case of the 144,000, the symbolism comes from the twelve tribes of Israel and the idea of fullness in the number 1000. The twelve tribes represent all God's people and also call to mind how God made for Himself a people from those who were once slaves in Egypt and gave them a land they had not earned or deserved. Remember what God told Moses to tell the people in Deuteronomy:

> And when the LORD your God brings you into the land that He swore to your fathers, to Abraham, to Isaac, and to Jacob, to give you—with great and good cities that you did not build, and houses full of all good things that you did not fill, and cisterns that you did not dig, and vineyards and olive trees that you did not plant—and when you eat and are full, then take care lest you forget the LORD, who brought you out of the land of Egypt, out of the house of slavery. It is the LORD your God you shall fear. Him you shall serve and by His name you shall swear. Deuteronomy 6:10–13

The twelve tribes remind us of how God has worked in history and that He will also give us the free gift of heaven.

If 144,000 is a symbolic number, why can't the six days of creation be symbolic and not literal?

It is important to notice that most of the numbers in the Bible are concrete, literal measurements. We only consider them symbolic when the context makes it clear that we are dealing with symbolic literature. The books of Revelation, Ezekiel, and Daniel are particularly symbolic books. If they are taken as literal history books rather than symbolic, they are misread. Everyone recognizes this to some degree, but strangely some groups take the numbers in Revelation very literally, believing, for instance, only 144,000 people will be saved or Christ will only rule His Church for 1000 years on earth (Revelation 20:4). Yet the same people understand that the archangel Michael did not come down from heaven with an actual chain and lock the devil down (Revelation 20:2). They pick and choose what is literal, such as the numbers, and what is figurative, such as Michael with a chain. The only way to read the Bible literally is to read it as it is written. Apocalyptic literature—which focuses on the end times—like the book of Revelation, is meant to be figurative.

On the other hand, Genesis is a historical account and description of how the universe came into being. In Genesis 1, the repetition of the phrase "and there was evening and there was morning" (verses 3, 8, 13, 19, 23, 31) along with the counting of the days shows us Moses meant this to be taken historically and literally, just as it is written. God uses the numbers six and seven to symbolize fullness and creation, but that symbolism is based in history, not fantasy. Think of the example of United States history used earlier. When we read in our history books that representatives of the thirteen colonies signed the Constitution of the United States in 1776, we know it is a historical fact. It is not just a convenient, symbolic number. But when there are thirteen candles on a Fourth of July party cake, we recognize it is symbolic of the original thirteen colonies. In the same way, the symbolic numbers of the Bible often take their cue from the historic ways God interacted with us according to His grace, but that doesn't mean they aren't literal or historic.

What about rounding? Read 1 Samuel 17:40. Why five stones?

It is possible that some numbers in the Bible were rounded off to an even number. The Bible says David picked up five smooth stones from the riverbank. Perhaps David reached down and grabbed a handful, and it happened that five of them filled his hand, no more or less. Or, in recording these events, Samuel rounded the number of stones David took to five in order to make it easier to follow.

The books of Moses were the most important part of the Bible at that time. Whatever else there was at the time of David (Job, maybe Judges) was understood to be commentary or interpretation of Moses. So the Word of God that gave David faith to face up to the giant Goliath came from the five books of Moses. David was acting like Abraham taking Isaac up the mountain (Genesis 22); Joseph in prison after Potiphar's wife's false charges (Genesis 39); or Moses leading the people in the wilderness without provisions (Exodus 16ff). David believed God would provide. David may well have grabbed exactly five stones, or it may have been a Spirit-guided rounding of the number by Samuel. Either way, the number of stones should help us see the connection between Goliath's defeat and Moses' writings. The connection is faith in God's promise to be faithful to us.

If the number was rounded, it was close. It is not as though David only took one stone from the river or took thirty. Rounding numbers is sometimes a convenient way to help readers obtain a better grasp of the event without getting caught in the details. Rounding can also help tie the event to other events and bring the number to bear symbolic importance. Despite the possibility of rounding, we never understand the numbers in the Bible to be a fabrication merely for the sake of making a point. So did David have exactly five stones in his pouch when he faced Goliath? We don't really know. It is certainly not impossible. But a literal reading of the Bible doesn't require it.

Read Exodus 12:37–38. How many people would that be with women and children? Is the Bible exaggerating?

In the Exodus passage above, the text itself says that the number of men was about 600,000. That "about" means this is not an exact number. It also means that it is close. We know this is a rounded number. We assume that it was rounded because it is easier to follow than if the author had told us an exact count of men, say, 597,654. It is rounded, but it has to be close. You can't round from 100,000 to 600,000.

But the number creates some problems. It is an incredibly huge number. If there was just one woman for each man and two children for each couple (and there were surely many more) the group that walked through the Red Sea on dry ground would have been 2.4 million Israelites. It was probably closer to twice this number. On top of the Israelites, there were the "mixed multitude" including Gentile servants who came with them. They also brought their flocks and herds. Imagine how many cattle and sheep 3 million people would need with them. This was an entire nation on the move. The logistics are almost impossible to imagine.

So is it an exaggeration to make a point? No! It was a miracle. These people were sustained by divine intervention. The entire event is miraculous. Imagine all the people in Houston walking at once across the Gulf of Mexico on dry land to Florida. The huge number of people isn't even the most spectacular part of this event.

Over the years, various scholars have tried to lessen the number of people in the Books of Exodus and Numbers to make them less dumbfounding, but none of the attempts are satisfactory. The Bible reports this as a literal number even though it is rounded. The context is the counting of heads, not visions of heaven. It is possible some evidence could arise showing we have somehow misread these numbers, but no error in translation or understanding will take away the awesome effect of moving an entire nation.

Symbolism of Specific Numbers

Earlier, we talked about some of the numbers repeated throughout the Scriptures, namely, three, seven, ten, twelve, and forty. Those numbers can all be divided and combined in consistent ways. This section will begin to explore this idea and will be repeated in part in future lessons. The chart the students fill out might also prove useful for future lessons.

Prime numbers and God's numbers

What are prime numbers? How might they be symbols of God?

A *prime number* is a positive integer that can only be divided by itself and one. The smaller numbers that divide into larger numbers are called "factors." Prime numbers symbolize sovereignty or immutability. They are made of nothing, factored by nothing. They are not divisible. Therefore they symbolize God, for God is indivisible, sovereign, and exists in perfection without anything or anyone else. The numbers one and three are especially symbolic of God, even though one is technically not a prime number. The number seven is also special to God. It is a prime number but is also a combined number. It combines the number of God (three) and the number of creation (four) and therefore represents fullness or completeness.

The Numbers of Creation

The number two and its multiples (even numbers) represent creation. Two is the number of Adam and Eve in the garden; there they are told to "multiply." Everything divisible by two is part of the creation. Even the animal kingdom knows this division so that also animals are male and female. Noah brought them on the ark by twos. When they left the ark, they also multiplied and filled the earth. Some biblical scholars argue that it is not two that is the basic building block, but four. There are four seasons and four cardinal directions or winds, north, south, east, and west. Four carries with it the idea of family in mother, father, son, and daughter.

How many "natures" does Christ have? What are they? How is it that this number embodies the mystery of the incarnation?

In the fullness of time, the Second Person of the Trinity, the Son, took up human flesh in the womb of the Virgin Mary and became a man. He now and forever has two natures—human and divine. He is fully God and fully man at the same time. The Father and the Spirit are also fully God. But they are not man. They have a divine nature but not a human. Thus, when Christ was joined to creation to be a sacrifice for the sins of the world, He took up the number of man within Himself. He has two natures. Yet because He is still and always also fully God, He also maintains God's number, for there are not two Christs, but only one. He is the only "two" that is not divisible. The Messiah's "numbers" are the number of man and the number of God combined in a wonderful mystery for our salvation. His unique combination of the numbers shows something of the mystery of God becoming man. These numbers will be more fully considered in the lessons which follow.

Numbers of Completion: Addition and Multiplication

What do seven, twelve, and ten, which we talked about earlier, symbolize?

By adding and multiplying the basic numbers, we get numbers that represent fullness or totality. Earlier we noted the number of God (three) plus the number of man (four) equals seven. Adding to this idea is the reality that seven is the number of days in the week. It is the days of creation (God created the universe in six days) plus the day of rest or the Sabbath. When Jesus points to Himself as the Sabbath, He is saying more than that He is our rest. He is also the completion of all things, the final piece in the new creation, the fullness of time and of God's purpose. By naming Himself as our Sabbath, Jesus takes claims that He is our completeness, or the totality of God (three) plus creation (four).

In the same way, the number of God (three) and the number of man (four) can be multiplied. Then we get the number twelve. Again the idea is completeness or fullness. Thus there are twelve tribes of Israel, twelve disciples, twelve baskets of fragments left over after the feeding of the five thousand, twenty-four elders ruling heaven (12 X 2 with twelve patriarchs representing the Old Testament and the twelve apostles representing the New Testament), and 144,000 saints in heaven (12 X 12 X 10^3).

The number five and the number ten are also numbers of completion. The number five is another way of combining God's number and man's number. You can arrive at the number five through the number of God (one) added to the number of creation and the family (four). As an alternate, five can be the number of God (three) and the number of man. There are five books of Moses, five stones in David's hand, and five books of the Psalms (The Psalter is divided into chapters 1–41; 42–72; 73–89; 90–106; and 107–150.).

Ten is five times two, or seven plus three. The Ten Commandments contain the full will and desire of God for our lives. Humans have ten fingers and toes. When numbers are multiplied by ten they represent fullness as well, such as the number one thousand (10 X 10 X 10). The number one thousand is a complete number (ten) to the power of God, 10^3. Thus Christ's reign on earth recorded in Revelation 20:4 should not be limited to a literal thousand years. Again, the idea is that one thousand means forever, a full completeness (ten) to the perfect power of God (three).

Numbers of Incompleteness

Read Revelation 13:18. Why 666? How does it relate to the numbers of God and to completion?

Many interpretations of this number have been put forth. The most satisfying to date is the idea that the number 666 typifies "the unholy trinity of the dragon (Revelation 12), the beast from the sea (13:1–10), and religious beast from the earth (13:11–18)" (*Concordia Commentary: Revelation*, p. 363). That idea places the number firmly in the context of John's vision and takes into account why there are three sixes instead of merely one. The wisdom called for to understand and calculate this number is simply "the wisdom that comes from God and enables the Christian to know and understand what this unholy trinity is and represents at any given time here on earth. This wisdom enables the Christian to discern how the evil forces of the dragon, both secular and religious, are always and everywhere active, at war to destroy the church and her witness to Christ" (*Concordia Commentary: Revelation*, p.363).

So the number 666 is symbolic—not magic. There is nothing to be afraid of in it. At the end of the day, it is only a number. There is no power in this number and there is nothing evil in having 666 as a street address or telephone or locker number. In John's vision, the number is meant to demonstrate the reality of evil.

But why this particular number? Even though it is a number of men, is divisible, and has many factors, it also might be meant to convey the idea of frustration. Instead of reading the number as 666 we can read the number as .666. The frustrating decimal .666 is arrived at by dividing three into two. The answer is not a solid .666. Rather it is a never-ending .6666666¯. If you multiply .666 X 3 to try and get back to 2, you can't. It is only 1.998. It is forever broken. It doesn't matter how many decimal points you use. Once you have divided 2 by 3 you can never get back. So it is incomplete by itself. And it is frustrated in its constant move outward, always moving but never really drawing any nearer to fullness and completeness. Not even our calculators or super computers can fix it. It is an impossible number. So also there might be here the idea that the number is not so much .666¯ as it is 6 2/3, which makes it 6.66666666¯. It is almost seven. The number represents anything in creation, whether an angel like the devil or a man, trying to be God but being essentially unable to fulfill the job and winding up as an exasperating parody of the full complete goodness of God.

Whatever we say about this strange number is bound to be somewhat speculative. This simply isn't one of the clearest passages in the Bible. But it should be made clear to the students that there is nothing dangerous about this number, we have nothing to fear, and we should not be superstitious about it.

God Wants Us to Do the Math

Read Matthew 18:21–22. How many times should we forgive our brother? Why doesn't Jesus do the math for Peter? Why doesn't He just say 490 times?

This example helps us to see that God sometimes uses numbers in a symbolic way based on their factors. God would not have us forgive our brother a mere 7 X 7 X 10 or 490 times. He would have us forgive our brother forever. Jesus demonstrates that this number is symbolic by speaking of it in terms of its factors. Rather than saying "490" He says "seventy times seven." Christ wants us to do more than the math. He wants us to see that the number is threefold, that it is a full number. We should notice also that He chooses seven. As we discussed earlier, both seven and ten are numbers of completion. The number seven particularly carries the idea of divine will and creation and ten of the Commandments. God's will and creation is to forgive transgressions against the Commandments. The meaning then is clearly not literal. Jesus does not teach that we should forgive our brother 490 times and then never again. By means of this symbolic number and its factors, he teaches that we should forgive him forever, or that we should forgive him until there are no more sins to forgive, until it is completely finished, as full as 7 X 7 X 10.

Because of the completeness of this number, there is also the idea here that the number should not be broken. So that every time we forgive our brother we do not subtract one, but rather we start back at zero again. How many more chances does my brother have after the first sin, after I have forgiven him one time? 489? No, 490! Seventy times seven. How many times after I have forgiven him 232 times? It is still 490 times. It never ends. That is the forgiveness we receive from God and it means that what Jesus teaches here is the same as He has taught us in the Lord's Prayer.

The numbers in the Bible do more than measure or count things. They show us that God cares about the details and they help to reveal something of God's perfect love for us in Jesus Christ. They also help to tie the various historical events together and remind us of who Jesus is for us. Numbers alone cannot convey the Gospel, the Good News of the forgiveness we have in Jesus. But, if they are taken seriously, they can help to open the Scriptures for us, and the student who learns to pay attention to them will find comfort through them.

Closing Prayer

We praise You, God; Your name we bless
And worship You in humbleness;
From day to day we glorify
Our everlasting God on high.
Of Your great glory do we sing,
And to Your throne our thanks we bring.

("All Glory Be to God Alone," *LSB* 948:2; *LW* 210:2)

The Counting God

God Counts and Biblical Numbers

What are some common numbers in the Bible? Are there any patterns?

Symbolism Based in History

Do numbers mean more than what they count? What do the numbers 1776 and 1492 mean to you? What about thirteen stripes and fifty stars on an American flag? How many shots in a twenty-one gun salute? What does it mean?

God Counts in Love

Read **Genesis 1:1–2:3.** How are the days counted? How does this relate to Sunday morning worship?

Read **Matthew 10:28–31**. What does this tell us about God?

Read again the familiar words of **John 3:16**. How does God love you? What does the word *so* mean in the phrase *God so loved the world*?

Read **Luke 15:4–7**. How many sheep are there? How does the shepherd know?

Read **Ezekiel chapters 40–41**. How many times does the word *cubit* occur? How about *rod*? What numbers are mentioned? What else? Why are the measurements so precise?

God Counts the Innumerable

Read **Psalm 40**. What is the number of God's merciful works? What makes David sing? Pay special attention to **verses 11–13**. How many evils surround David? Who can count them? What is the familiar phrase in this psalm?

Sinners Count to Him

Read **Luke 7:37–39**. Think to yourself about Jesus' words about counting the hairs of our heads while you read this. How does that color what the woman does to our Lord's feet with her hair? Now read **Luke 7:44–50**.

An Introduction to the Symbolism of Biblical Numbers

Read **Revelation 7:4–9**. How many saints does John see? Notice the number in **verse 4** and the number in **verse 9**. What are some clues that this is a symbolic number and not literal? What are its factors? And what does this tell us about how many people will be in heaven?

If 144,000 is a symbolic number, why can't the six days of creation be symbolic and not literal?

What about rounding? Read **1 Samuel 17:40**. Why five stones?

Read **Exodus 12:37–38**. How many people would that be with women and children? Is the Bible exaggerating?

Key Numbers

1	2	5
3		10
	4	12
7		40

Symbolism of Specific Numbers

Prime Numbers and God's Numbers

What are prime numbers? How might they be symbols of God?

The Numbers of Creation

How many "natures" does Christ have? What are they? How is it that this number embodies the mystery of the Incarnation?

Numbers of Completion: Addition and Multiplication

What do seven, twelve, and ten, which we talked about earlier, symbolize?

Numbers of Incompleteness

Read **Revelation 13:18**. Why this number? How does it relate to the numbers of God and to completion?

God Wants Us to Do the Math

Read **Matthew 18:21–22**. How many times should we forgive our brother? Why doesn't Jesus do the math for Peter? Why doesn't He just say 490 times?

2

THREE-IN-ONE: THE NUMBER OF GOD

Lesson Focus

One of the greatest and most essential articles of faith is a number! The word *Trinity* means "three-in-one." We use it to talk about who God is and also to define who God isn't. But Trinity doesn't quite add up—three-in-one is mathematical nonsense. The wisdom of God is foolishness to mankind, so this "nonsense" is deliberate. This mathematical impossibility helps us to confess a mystery that numbers and words cannot express. Our minds cannot contain it. This lesson will use the numbers one and three to show how the Bible reveals both God's essential being and His character.

Opening Prayer

Almighty and everlasting God, since You have given us, Your servants, grace to acknowledge the glory of the eternal Trinity by the confession of a true faith, and to worship the Unity in the power of Your divine majesty, keep us also steadfast in this true faith and worship, and defend us ever from all our adversaries; for You, O Father, Son, and Holy Spirit, live and reign, one God, now and forever. Amen.

(Collect for Trinity Sunday, *LW*, p.61)

The Name of God: The ONE

What is a prime number? What are the lowest prime numbers you can think of? What about the number one? Is it prime? How is it unique?

A prime number is a real number, a positive integer, that is divisible only by itself and one. The first prime numbers in numeric order are three, five, seven, eleven, and thirteen.

Technically, the number one is not a prime number. One is only divisible by itself. It is not prime, but it is the most unique of all numbers. It is also foundational to all counting and arithmetic. All numbers are built upon and are divisible by one. In the Bible, prime numbers symbolize God or divine completeness. We'll deal with the number seven in a later lesson. Other than three the other prime numbers are not commonly found in Scripture.

The number one is the number of God. Even as the number one doesn't quite fit into our patterns (prime and non-prime) so also God is unique. He does not fit into, indeed is not part of, creation. No created being is one. Nothing created can make that claim since everything in creation is related to and dependent on other things. Everything in creation affects and is affected by other things in creation. God has not created anything that exists alone or that *can* exist alone. Only God is one. He is the only one who is sovereign, who is autonomous, who doesn't need anything or anyone else, and who has no source. There are no other gods. There is no other one. In the divine name, we will see there are not even any other things, there is only God. He is One.

Read Exodus 3:13–17. What words are in all caps? What name does God give Moses in verse 14? How is that name like the number one?

Consider the verb *to be* in English as shown below. If God speaks of Himself as "I AM," what should we call Him?

to be	Singular	Plural
1st person	I am	We are
2nd person	You are	You are
3rd person	He is	They are

Have you ever seen the Hebrew word *YHWH* before? What does it mean?

The first thing we ought to notice about this strange name is that it is a verb. He is the one who is. He is the one who will be. The verb *to be* is the most complicated and most important word in every language. If you can't say or express the idea of being you can't say or express anything. *To be* is the foundational verb. When God tells Moses that His name is "I AM WHO I AM" He is saying a lot about His nature. His name implies the number one, for He is the one who is. The verb *to be* stands in similar relationship to other words as One does to other numbers—it is always a factor.

Notice that God gives His name to Moses in the first person. He says: "I AM WHO I AM" or "I WILL BE WHO I WILL BE." The first person is "I." He does not give His name in the third person "he." (Refer to chart.) In Exodus 3 the person shifts from "I" to "He" in verse 15. In Hebrew, the new name for God is *hwhy*. We can represent this with the English letters *YHWH*. You may have seen those Hebrew letters before on stoles or paraments, as symbols in Church. They are God's personal name. It is translated "He is."

Consider if I said to you "I am David." If you were talking to me and wanted to express the same reality you would not say, "I am David," you would say, "You are David." If you were talking about me you'd say, "He is David." Hebrew has similar rules. Moses can't say "I AM" any more than you would say, "I am David" (unless that is your name). So God's name changes in Exodus from "I AM" to "HE IS." That is the way we refer to Him.

St. Paul wrote, "In Him we live and move and have our being" (Acts 17:28). How does that relate to the name God spoke from the burning bush?

This is also related to the shift from first person to third (see chart and paragraph above). God's name means that He is. Nothing else is. He is the only one. Pharaoh is not. We are not. Nothing else is. Only God is. He is, and that is it. In Him, we live and move and have our being. In Him is everything that lives and moves and has its being. There is no living, no moving, no being apart from Him. Consider the passages earlier about the care of sparrows and grooming of lilies. God is. Since He is, we aren't.

Read Exodus 3:14–17 again. God is, but so what? How is He known? Where is He? Who is He?

God is not an abstraction. He is not an idea. God is not floating around in outer space all alone, simply being, all by Himself. He is in His creation. In God all things live and move and have their being. He is active in history. He is the God of Abraham, of Isaac, and of Jacob. He is the God who will rescue His people out of Egypt from all these enemies, the Canaanites, the Hittites, and the like. He will deliver them to a land flowing with milk and honey. God is in His actions: creating, sustaining, providing, speaking, sending, and rescuing. He worked and spoke through Moses, just as He had worked and spoken through the patriarchs before Moses, just as He works to this day through the hands of men.

The LORD

Look at Exodus 3:15 one more time. Who is Moses to say sent him? What name is Moses to use for the God of Abraham? How does that word look different than the other words?

This special, personal name of God, *YHWH*, is indicated in modern English translations by the word *LORD* in small caps. In the King James translation it is translated *Jehovah*. When we see *LORD* in the text in all caps we know that the Hebrew word *YHWH* is the root of that word. Through the prophet, psalmist, or historian who recorded these words of Scripture, God is speaking in a very personal way. He is using the divine personal name, the name given to Moses from the burning bush. It is a name revealed only to His people. All humanity knows innately that there is a "god." The Gentiles, who do not know

God, show that the work of the Law is written on their hearts. Their consciences bear witness against them. Even without the revealed Word of God, their thoughts conflict with their actions, so that they either accuse themselves or excuse themselves, but in either case they know there is a right and wrong (Romans 2:15). But this name, *Lord*, does not mean some generic, half-known god of the law. This is the name of God revealed in mercy. This is the God who is, the God who will deliver us. When we see this name in the Bible or hear the title "Lord," it should invoke in us the remembrance that God liberated His people from Egypt and has promised to make us His people and be our God. He is the only one who can be, the only one who is. Whoever holds the faith and hope of Abraham is Abraham's true son, and Abraham's Lord is also his Lord. "Abraham 'believed God, and it was counted to him as righteousness'? Know then that it is those of faith who are the sons of Abraham" (Galatians 3:6–7).

The name *YHWH* or *Lord* always conveys this special honor and privilege due to God alone. He is One.

Read Psalm 23 silently. Do you see the word *Lord* in capital letters? What then does that tell us about who the Shepherd is and in whose house we shall dwell? Spend a few minutes looking around in the Old Testament. Can you find any more places where God's divine name is used?

For many individuals, Psalm 23 is a most well-loved Scripture. Most see the beauty in this psalm without even fully realizing its context. But when we learn to see the divine name, Lord, the psalm takes on the context of God's salvation history. The Lord is my Shepherd. He is the one who spoke to Moses from the burning bush, the God who is. He brought His people out of slavery. We will dwell in the house of the Lord, of the one who is, forever. Because He is, He has power and authority to make it so. He causes our cup to overflow with blessing and confounds our enemies. He is the one who loves us. Our Shepherd is not just any god. He is the one, true, and only God.

Whenever we see small caps, we know that *YHWH* is the word behind *Lord*. God is speaking in an intimate, personal way, and we see more deeply the grace of God.

Have the students thumb around a little bit so they learn to see how the word Lord is used throughout the Old Testament.

Read Ezekiel 37:3 and Genesis 2:7. Which passage has "Lord God" and which one has "Lord God"? What is the difference?

In the Ezekiel passage, the English text renders *God* in capital letters instead of Lord. In the Genesis passage, *Lord* is in capital letters and God is in lowercase letters. In the Ezekiel passage, the Hebrew is *Lord YHWH*. If it were translated "Lord Lord" it would be very confusing. So this unique construction is rendered Lord God. The capital letters of *God* indicate that it is *YHWH*, the personal divine name and the lowercase letters of "Lord" indicate the Hebrew word for *lord*. In the Genesis passage, the word *Lord* is capitalized to translate the divine name, *YHWH*. The word *God* in lowercase letters here is the Hebrew word *Elohim*. *Elohim* is a more generic word for God. It is similar to the English word *god*. It could be used of false gods. But *YHWH* is only used for the true, living God of Abraham, the One revealed through the prophets and confirmed in Jesus Christ. So small capitals indicate the divine name even when the word is *God* and not *Lord*.

Why the word *Lord* instead of a translation of the name like "He is"? Why not just write the Hebrew word in English letters like *YHWH* or *Yahweh*?

In the first place, the verb *to be* is not a very practical name. Verbs don't make good names. Imagine if a person had the English verb *He runs* as a name. Imagine sentences like: *He runs* went to the store for some bread. *He runs* is tall. *He runs* eats and runs. That sounds ridiculous. But imagine if it were the verb *to be*. That is even worse: *He is* is not having a good day. *He is* was late for school. If YHWH was translated "He is," it would be very confusing. Imagine: *He is* is a jealous God. *He is* is good. But that ridiculousness is a large part of why God uses this name. He is unlike any other and *He is*. He chooses a name for Himself that is the foundation block of all language. The verb *to be* is the most fundamental word of all language. It is all encompassing. It is a bold claim. He is the one who is. But as revealing as that name is, it is not very practical. If it were translated each time, it would be hard to follow. It would sound like every sentence with God's name had two verbs.

Besides being potentially confusing, God's people have usually not translated this name or spoken it out loud. Substituting *LORD* instead of using *YHWH* or *HE IS* is following the custom handed to us. The rabbinic tradition by the time of Jesus Christ was that no believer should ever speak the Lord's personal name out loud. It was never to be said. They refrained from speaking the name *YHWH* lest the name somehow be inadvertently misused and the second commandment broken. Whenever *YHWH* appeared in written text, the Jews would read out loud "Adonai," that is, the Hebrew word that is translated "Lord." Our translations follow this tradition.

How does Luther direct us to use God's name in his explanation to the Second Commandment? How does that shed light on the use of the divine name *YHWH*?

We don't want to judge the piety of our forefathers. But there was a grave danger in this approach. The Law does not merely demand that God's name not be misused. It also demands it be used. The Second Commandment has both a positive and a negative use. Remember Luther's explanation to the Second Commandment, "You shall not misuse the name of the Lord your God. We should fear and love God so that we do not curse, swear, use satanic arts, lie, or deceive by His name, but call upon it in every trouble, pray, praise, and give thanks" (Small Catechism). Luther exhorts us to call upon God's name in every trouble, pray, praise, and give thanks. We must use God's name as He has given it to us. Failing to use God's name is just as much of a sin as misusing it. Still, there is something powerful about God's most personal name. We would do well not to use it lightly.

In Mark 12:29, Jesus quotes Deuteronomy 6:4. Read both passages. Do you see capital letters in Deuteronomy? How is *LORD* translated in Mark? Any caps?

Mark simply has "Lord"; only the first letter is capitalized. The Greek text has no special indicator. But this convinces us to stick with "Lord" in the Old Testament instead of translating or transliterating *YHWH*. It is, as already mentioned, the rabbinic tradition and reasoning. But more importantly, we see here divine approval. The Greek New Testament does not translate the divine name as "He is." Following the Septuagint (the Greek translation of the Hebrew Old Testament), it simply renders the Hebrew name as *kyrios*, which is "Lord." This guides our English Bibles in the Old Testament. Since the inspired writers translated YHWH as *kyrios* (*lord* in Greek) we follow that tradition also in our translations of the Old Testament. But we make a distinction. If the translation is from Hebrew we use small caps.

Jesus Is the LORD

How do we read *YHWH* in the New Testament without small caps?

Once we know that *LORD* in the Old Testament and *Lord* in the New Testament refer back to God's personal name, it does more than tell us how to translate. It shows us that the One who spoke to Moses from the bush that burned but was not consumed and sent Moses to Pharaoh to liberate His people is the One who was born of Mary. Jesus is Lord. The Christian Church addresses Jesus as Lord not as a sign merely that He is the Ruler of the Universe, but that He is the God of Abraham, Moses, and Jacob. The greatest claim that Jesus Himself makes to this name and oneship is during the trial by Caiaphas.

> **Read Luke 22:66–71. What has this to do with the name *LORD*? What is it about Jesus' answer that causes Caiaphas to react so violently? Is it simply that He agreed that He is the Son of God, or does it have something to do with the form of His answer? Read John 11:49–53. How does Caiaphas use his prophecy to trap Jesus in Luke 22?**

Our Lord's response echoes the name from the burning bush. If Jesus answered in Hebrew, He said "Yahweh" out loud, and broke the rabbinic tradition. There is no other way to say, "I AM" in Hebrew. But even worse than saying God's name out loud and breaking some man-made rule, Jesus was claiming this most sacred name for Himself. He claims to be the only One who is! It was a perfect excuse for Caiaphas to make a fuss.

Caiaphas led Jesus into this answer. John shares Caiaphas's prophecy that Jesus would die for the people (John 11:51). Caiaphas saw Jesus merely as the scapegoat or "fall guy" for the Jewish nation. In Caiaphas's view, Jesus' death would satisfy the Romans by settling down the tension and unrest building within the populace.

Jesus acknowledges Caiaphas's prophecy, but from an entirely different perspective. He knew it was better for Him to die than for mankind to perish for all eternity. He walked into the trap with His eyes open. Think of how often our Lord prophesied His crucifixion:

> And He began to teach them that the Son of Man must suffer many things and be rejected by the elders and the chief priests and the scribes and be killed, and after three days rise again. (Mark 8:31)

> The Son of Man must suffer many things and be rejected by the elders and chief priests and scribes, and be killed, and on the third day be raised. (Luke 9:22)

> But first He must suffer many things and be rejected by this generation. (Luke 17:25)

> Was it not necessary that the Christ should suffer these things and enter into His glory? (Luke 24:26)

> [Jesus] said to them, "Thus it is written, that the Christ should suffer and on the third day rise from the dead." (Luke 24:46)

Jesus was chosen to die for the sins of the world. Neither Caiaphas nor Pilate nor Pilate's men killed Him. He laid down His life of His own accord. He made Himself a sacrifice not only for Israel, but also for the entire world and all time. It was the most expedient event of all time, the best thing for humanity that has ever happened.

In the trial before Caiaphas, Jesus clearly identifies Himself. He is the One who sent Moses to free His people from Egypt and lead them into the Promised Land. He is "I AM." He came and endured Caiaphas's hatred even as He would endure the scourge of Pilate's men to make good on the promise from the burning bush. To this day, the angel of death passes over those marked with His blood. For Christians, death is merely temporal; they will live forever with their Savior. Jesus is the one, the only one, who is. He rightly takes the name from the burning bush as His own. The reaction of Caiaphas is no better than that of Pharaoh. His heart is hard. He feigns outrage and goes about his evil plan. But, as in the case of Joseph, God works the evil intended by men for good. "As for you, you meant evil against me, but God meant it for good, to bring it about that many people should be kept alive, as they are today" (Genesis 50:20).

The Holy Trinity

What is wrong with the sentence, "Hear, O Israel: the Lord our Gods is one Lord." How does it read in Deuteronomy 6:4?

That passage certainly bears witness to the unity of God, to the number one. But there is a problem. The first sentence, where the word *Gods* is plural, is literal. You won't find it that way in an English Bible. They have all corrected the Hebrew! Why? If they translated it literally it would sound like nonsense, just like it does above. How can the Lord be Gods (plural) if He is one? How can He be one if He is Gods? The verse sounds contradictory. Not only does it not make logical sense, it is also grammatically incorrect. The verb *is* is singular and the noun *Gods* is plural. It is just as bad in Hebrew as it is in English. It is like saying "The boy our sons are one kid." It does not fit with our reason or grammar. Translated literally it reads: "the HE IS our Gods is one HE IS." This isn't an obscure passage. In fact, it was a kind of Old Testament creed. The Jewish tradition, still carried on today, was to say this verse as a prayer every morning and evening.

How can we understand the "bad grammar" of Deuteronomy 6:4 or the idea that God is three in one?

We can't. This is not something we can understand. The problem is not with the reality of the Trinity. The problem is the limits of our minds, words, and numbers. The Father, the Son, and the Holy Spirit is one Lord. That is not a typo. "Is" is right. It is not "are" because He is one. What jars our ears is not bad grammar or illogical counting. It is the mystery of the Holy Trinity. This is not something we can understand. It is something we believe. The numbers in the Old Testament confess the mysterious threefold plurality within the unity of the Godhead by showing how numbers fail, how our reason and language fail. What cannot be true mathematically, what words cannot fully express, what we cannot understand, is still true. God is three. God is one. There is no contradiction.

Read the first section of the Athanasian Creed, which is traditionally used on Trinity Sunday, printed below. According to this, what can we say about the Trinity? What must we say?

Athanasian Creed:

Whoever will be saved shall, above all else, hold the catholic faith.

Which faith, except everyone keeps whole and undefiled, without doubt he will perish eternally.

And the catholic faith is this, that we worship one God in three persons and three persons in one God, neither confusing the persons nor dividing the substance.

For there is one person of the Father, another of the Son, and another of the Holy Spirit.

But the Godhead of the Father, of the Son, and of the Holy Spirit is all one: the glory equal, the majesty coeternal. (*LW*, p. 134)

We must say there is only one God. He is three persons—Father, Son, and Holy Spirit. Those three persons are all equally God. They all hear and answer prayers. They all love us. They all created the world, redeemed the world, and sanctify us. But they are not the same. They are three distinct persons. There are not three Gods—only one. The distinctions between the persons of the Trinity are internal. The Father is not the Son or the Holy Spirit. The Father is not begotten. He does not proceed. The Son is begotten of the Father only and does not proceed. The Holy Spirit is not begotten, but proceeds from the Father and the Son. Confusing? Yes. It is not a matter of intellect, but of faith. The Scriptures bear witness to this reality in passages such as Deuteronomy 6:4. We can read it and believe it, but this side of heaven we cannot understand it.

Jesus the One

Read Romans 5:5–21. What is the role of each of the persons in the Trinity in this section of Scripture? How is the word *one* used differently throughout this passage?

The One who died at the right time for the ungodly, the Son, is the Father's love poured into our hearts by the Holy Spirit. The One who gave His life to make us His is the three-in-one. Throughout this section of Romans the word *one* is used in different ways. It refers to any human in verse 7. In verses 12 and 15, it is Adam. In verse 14, it is Christ. In verses 17–18, it is Adam in the first instance and Christ in the second. The idea is that one man, Adam, infected all men with his sin. So a new and greater "Adam" (*man* in Hebrew) came along who did what the first Adam should have done. He stood between the tempter and Eve. He protected her and took her blame. He laid down His life to save her. This One made all men clean. He reconciled all men to His Father. He put an end to death's reign and gave life as a free gift to all men. Ultimately it is not Adam who is one. It is Jesus. He is the one who defines mankind. He is the One who brings them to eternal life.

Read Hebrews 7:11–27. Who is the one made a priest without an oath? Who is the one who said to Him, "The Lord has sworn . . ."? What was the number of the former priests? What is different about the order of Melchizedek? What is the significance of a sacrifice offered up "once for all"?

In this important passage, we hear the oneness of Jesus being tied closely to His uniqueness. The "one of whom these things are spoken" (verse 13) and the one "who has become a priest" (verse 16) is Jesus. He is not a priest after the Levitical priesthood. He is not of the house of Aaron. He does not follow the ceremonial law of Moses (verse 11) but is a law unto Himself (verse 12). The order of Melchizedek (Genesis 14:18) is older than the order of Aaron (Numbers 3:3). Melchizedek ministered to Abraham. The "former" priests of Hebrews 7:23 were "many in number" because they kept dying and couldn't be priests forever. But Jesus is a priest forever in the order of Melchizedek (verse 17, quoting Psalm 110:4). The Father spoke these anointing words to Jesus when John baptized Jesus, "This is My beloved Son in whom I am well-pleased." He is the one who swore to the Son, and in the promise that He would be a priest forever is hidden the promise that He will rise from the dead. For our great High Priest Jesus is the only one who could offer a sacrifice in Himself that is worthy of all the sins of all men and who could also overcome death. Thus His sacrifice is the one sacrifice, the one that ends and completes all sacrifice and opens heaven to all believers.

Divine Geometry

Look at the diagram below. How does the symbolism of numbers come into play?

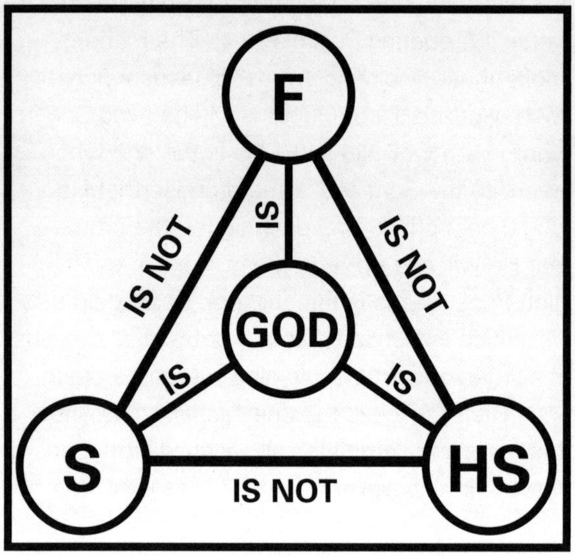

Geometry can also take on the symbolism of numbers. Four is the number of creation (lesson 3), so the earth is described as though it were a square, with four sides and four corners (Genesis 2:10; Revelation 7:1), even though we know it is round. Even as squares are made of four lines, circles are made of one continuous line. Thus the circle is a symbol of divinity. The triangle, with three sides and three corners, can be a symbol of God.

In the chart, the circles at the points of the triangle, in the middle, represent the Three Persons of the Holy Trinity: the Father, the Son, and the Holy Spirit. On the side of the triangle, where one Person is connected to the other, it should say "is not." The Father is equal to the Son and the Holy Spirit, but He is neither the Son nor the Holy Spirit. This is true of all three persons. The circle in the middle should say "God." The lines that go from each person to the circle in the middle should say "is." The Father is God, the Son is God, and the Holy Spirit is God. Of course God can't be reduced to geometry. It is merely a symbol meant to convey some of what we confess about the Trinity. That is why the entire thing is inside of a rectangle. The rectangle, with its four sides and four corners, represents the world and time. It is like we are looking through a window. Even though God is outside of time, we are not. Everything we know about God we know from within these physical constraints and reality.

The Threefold God in Praise and Blessing

Read Isaiah 6:1–7. How many threes are there? Does this sound familiar?

Look at the capitalization of the word *Lord* in verse 1 as compared to verses 3 and 5. What does that tell us? In verse 1, Isaiah uses the generic word for *Lord.* But the seraphim sing the precise praise to the revealed God of Abraham.

The angels called seraphim each have three pairs of wings. They use one set of wings to fly. The other two sets are for covering their shame, that is, their feet and their eyes; for God's holiness is so great even they are hesitant to look upon Him. The praise they sing is threefold: "Holy, Holy, Holy." This threefold praise is not accidental. They are responding in praise to the threefold character of God, one *holy* for each Person. Their praise reflects the character of God. He is one, yet He is three. Their three pairs of wings make them unlike any flying creature on earth. It also reflects something of the threefold character of God's holiness.

Read Revelation 4:1–14. How many sets of three are listed here? What song do they sing? How many different numbers are given and what do they mean?

The vision of St. John is similar to Isaiah's vision. These four beasts also have three sets of wings and sing the same song as the seraphim. They are also said to give glory, honor, and thanks to the One who sits on the throne. We are going to deal with some of these other numbers later, but the number of elders is twenty-four. That is three times eight, or three times four times two. Those twenty-four represent the patriarchs or tribes of the Old Testament and the apostles of the New Testament. Four is a number of creation. Multiplying three times four indicates fullness. We'll have more to say about this later, but it is good to see how similar it is to the Isaiah vision and to notice that the song in heaven is still the same, and that it is deliberately threefold.

The song sounds familiar because we sing this angelic song in the Communion Liturgy. It is called the Sanctus. That is Latin for *holy*. We sing it right before the consecration and the reception of Holy Communion along with the Palm Sunday praise, "Hosanna in the highest. Blessed is He who comes in the name of the Lord." We believe that the One the angels praised in the heavenly temple as seen in Isaiah's vision, and the One worshiped and praised by the four strange creatures in John's vision is present for us in our churches. He comes to us in the flesh, born of Mary, crucified, and raised from the dead in order to forgive our sins and join us to Him. He rides into our churches not on a donkey, but in lowly bread and wine. We sing "Holy, Holy, Holy" as a confession that, even if the world can't see Him, this is the one who purged Isaiah's unclean lips. He will do the same for us. All three persons of the Holy Trinity are present in our worship. So we sing "Holy" for each of them.

Read Numbers 6:22–27. Do you see any threes? Does this sound familiar? Don't forget to notice the capital letters! What do those capital letters have to do with the promise at the end: "they will put My name upon the people of Israel and I will bless them"? Where is God's name put on us?

The Lutheran tradition, started by Luther himself, is to have the pastor pronounce this blessing on the congregation at the end of the Divine Service. The blessing God tells Moses to tell the priests to say over the people is threefold, "The LORD bless . . . ; the LORD make His . . . ; the LORD lift up . . . and give you peace" (Numbers 6:24–26). The Old Testament priests were to announce the blessing of the Holy Trinity. They spoke that blessing onto the people at the LORD's command and with the LORD's promise.

This is a special blessing in the Scriptures. It is special because it has a promise attached to it. God said to Moses: "So shall they (the Old Testament priests) put My name upon the people of Israel, and I will bless them." The name that the priests put upon them is YHWH, the LORD. Notice that in English the word *LORD* at the beginning of each phrase is capitalized. If that name is upon you, you belong to Him. You have His grace, His peace, and His promise.

The promise was specific to the Old Testament priests. But Martin Luther adapted it for the Divine Service. Luther was emboldened to do this because even though God didn't tell him to have the pastors use this blessing the way He had Moses tell the Old Testament priests, we have an even greater name placed on us. God put His fullest, most personal name on us in Holy Baptism. We were baptized into YHWH when we were baptized into the name of the Father and of the Son and of the Holy Spirit.

Read Matthew 28:16–20. There are no capital letter words! What is the name of Baptism? How does this relate to YHWH? What are the promises in these verses?

The name of Baptism is the fullest name of God, the Father, the Son, and the Holy Spirit. This revelation only came after the Second Person of the Holy Trinity took on our flesh in the virgin's womb. God now has a human name—Jesus. That is the Greek form of the Hebrew name *Joshua*. He is the LORD who saves His people. You can see YHWH in the "Jo" of Joshua. The other part of the name is the word "to save" (*yasha*). The angel Gabriel tells Joseph to name his son Jesus in Matthew 1:21. He explains the meaning of the name. He is to save His people. Once God has a human name, a human body and soul, the revelation of God is greater. The New Testament revelation is not different in content than the Old Testament, but it is fuller. God is more intimate with us now that He shares our humanity. He is with us, is one of us, and the prophecy spoken by Isaiah is fulfilled. He is our Immanuel. The name God has given is more fully and obviously threefold as well: He is the one who is and will be, He is the Father, the Son, and the Holy Spirit.

Sometimes these verses at the end of Matthew are called the Great Commission. These are the last things Jesus says to His disciples before ascending into heaven forty days after the resurrection. He gave the disciples this command: "Go therefore and make disciples of all nations" (28:19). But that is only a small part of the verses. That command to *go* and *make* is set in the midst of a promise. Jesus says, "All authority in heaven and on earth has been given to Me" (28:18). That is what *therefore* refers to. Because Jesus has all authority, the disciples are to go. He has the authority and the power to make it work. The apostles won't really make disciples. Jesus will. He will make disciples by His authority over all things in heaven and on earth. He will make disciples through Holy Baptism into His name and by the teaching that He has given to, and that He will do through, the apostles. The apostles weren't sent out to figure it out, or to make it work by their own authority. They were sent with the clear promise that God would do what He says. Following the command, there is another promise: "I am with you always to the end of the age" (28:20). Not only does Jesus have the authority, but He is not sending them out alone. Jesus, the Authoritative One, His Father and the Spirit, will be there. He will do the work. He will keep His Word.

Closing Prayer

All glory be to God alone,
Forevermore the highest one.
Who did our sinful race befriend;
And grace and peace to us extend.
Among us may His gracious will,
All hearts with deep thanksgiving fill.
You only are the Holy One
And over all are Lord alone.
O Jesus Christ, we glorify
You and the Spirit, Lord Most High;
With Him You evermore shall be
One in the Father's majesty.

("All Glory Be to God Alone," *LSB* 948:1; 5 *LW* 210:1, 5)

Three-in-One: The Number of God

The Name of God: The ONE

What is a prime number? What are the lowest prime numbers you can think of? What about the number one? Is it prime? How is it unique?

Read **Exodus 3:13–17**. What words are in all caps? What name does God give Moses in **verse 14**? How is that name like the number one?

Consider the verb *to be* in English as shown below. If God speaks of Himself as "I am," what should we call Him?

to be	Singular	Plural
1st person	I am	We are
2nd person	You are	You are
3rd person	He is	They are

Have you ever seen the Hebrew word YHWH before? What does it mean?

St. Paul wrote, "In Him we live and move and have our being" **(Acts 17:28)**. How does that relate to the name God spoke from the burning bush?

Read **Exodus 3:14–17** again. God is, but so what? How is He known? Where is He? Who is He?

The LORD

Look at **Exodus 3:15** one more time.

Who is Moses to say sent him? What name is Moses to use for the God of Abraham? How does that word look different than the other words?

Read **Psalm 23** silently. Do you see the word LORD in capital letters? What then does that tell us about who the Shepherd is and in whose house we shall dwell? Spend a few minutes looking around in the Old Testament. Can you find any more places where the Divine name is used?

Read **Ezekiel 37:3** and **Genesis 2:7**. Which passage has "Lord GOD" and which one has "LORD God"? What is the difference?

Why the word *LORD* instead of a translation of the name like "He is"? Why not just write the Hebrew word in English letters like *YHWH* or *Yahweh*?

How does Luther direct us to use God's name in his explanation to the Second Commandment? How does that shed light on the use of the divine name *YHWH*?

In **Mark 12:29**, Jesus quotes **Deuteronomy 6:4**. Read both passages. Do you see capital letters in Deuteronomy? How is *LORD* translated in Mark? Any caps?

Jesus Is the LORD

How do we read *YHWH* in the New Testament without small caps?

Read **Luke 22:66–71**. What has this to do with the name *LORD*? What is it about Jesus' answer that causes Caiaphas to react so violently? Is it simply that He agreed that He is the Son of God, or does it have something to do with the form of His answer? Read **John 11:49–53**. How does Caiaphas use his prophecy to trap Jesus in **Luke 22**?

The Holy Trinity

What is wrong with the sentence: "Hear, O Israel: the LORD our God is one LORD"? How does it read in **Deuteronomy 6:4**?

How can we understand the "bad grammar" of Deuteronomy 6:4 or the idea that God is three in one?

Read the first section of the Athanasian Creed, which is traditionally used on Trinity Sunday, printed below. According to this, what can we say about the Trinity? What must we say?

Athanasian Creed

Whoever will be saved shall, above all else, hold the catholic faith.

Which faith, except everyone keeps whole and undefiled, without doubt he will perish eternally.

And the catholic faith is this, that we worship one God in three persons and three persons in one God, neither confusing the persons nor dividing the substance.

For there is one person of the Father, another of the Son, and another of the Holy Spirit.

But the Godhead of the Father, of the Son, and of the Holy Spirit is all one: the glory equal, the majesty coeternal. (*LW*, p. 134)

Jesus the One

Read **Romans 5:5–21**. What is the role of each of the persons in the Trinity in this section of Scripture? How is the word *one* used differently throughout this passage?

Read **Hebrews 7:11–27**. Who is the one made a priest without an oath? Who is the one who said to Him, "The Lord has sworn . . ."? What was the number of the former priests? What is different about the order of Melchizedek? What is the significance of a sacrifice offered up "once for all"?

Divine Geometry

Look at the diagram below. How does the symbolism of numbers come into play?

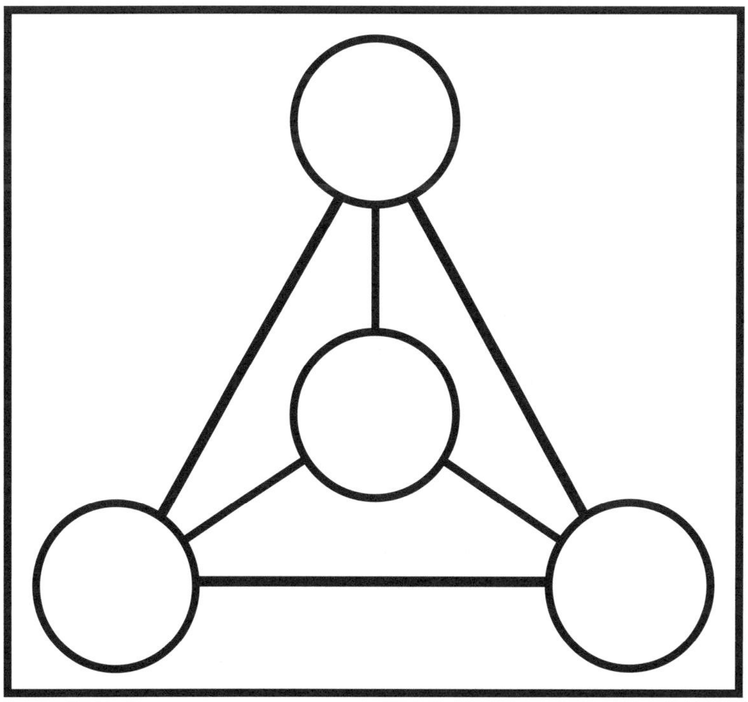

The Threefold God in Praise and Blessing

Read **Isaiah 6:1–7**. How many threes are there? Does this sound familiar? (Side note: Look at the capitalization of the word *Lord* in verse 1 as compared to verses 3 and 5. What does that tell us?)

Read **Revelation 4:1–14**. How many sets of three are listed here? What song do they sing? How many different numbers are given and what do they mean?

Read **Numbers 6:22–27**. Do you see any threes? Does this sound familiar? Don't forget to notice the capital letters! What do those capital letters have to do with the promise at the end: "they will put My Name upon the people of Israel and I will bless them"? Where is God's Name put on us?

Read **Matthew 28:16–20**. There are no capital letter words! What is the name of Baptism? How does this relate to YHWH? What are the promises in these verse

3

TWO AND FOUR: CREATION COUNTED

Lesson Focus

The numbers two and four were introduced to us in Lesson 1. They are numbers of men and of creation. Two is a prime number, the smallest and only even prime. Prime numbers always demonstrate a certain fullness. Two also indicates balance. With that balanced and even character, both two and four show a relationship or dependence on others. This lesson will begin to unpack the idea of relationship between men and animals on the basis of the number two in the Bible. Then we will explore the number four as it symbolizes the fullness of creation, not only on earth but also in heaven.

Opening Prayer:

Lord of my life, I ask Your blessing on my daily life and especially on my work. My work is good because Your hand is upon it. Do not let me turn my work to selfish purposes. Forgive me when I fail. Help me to remember that You are still Lord when I feel discouraged and useless or when I am tense and angry. Help me to remember You are still Lord when I am satisfied and pleased with my accomplishments. Take my work into Your own hands. Give blessing to all I do and say. Use what I accomplish as a blessing to others, for Jesus' sake. Amen.

(*Lutheran Book of Prayer,* p.180)

Man Is Never One, Never Alone

Read Ecclesiastes 4:7–12. What is the "vanity" that the author is writing about? What solution does he offer? Read Genesis 2:18–25. What is not good? Compare this text to the verses from Ecclesiastes.

Even the melancholy preacher of Ecclesiastes, so seemingly without hope, recognizes man cannot live alone. Life still might be in vain—it still might lead to dust—but man cannot live by himself. Two is better than one.

God saw that man should not be alone even

before the fall into sin. He proclaimed all things good except one thing. It was not good for man to be alone. Two are better than one. Even without the vanities of this sad life, without temptation and envy, without vice or sorrow, two was better than one. Even in Paradise, without toil or the threat of falling or getting cold or being attacked in any way, it was not good for Adam to be alone. Two is better than one.

Read Proverbs 17:17 and Proverbs 18:24. How do these verses reinforce this theme?

God, through the preacher in Ecclesiastes, tells us it is not good for man to be alone and two is better than one. We know this is true. We know how hard it is to be alone. Who hasn't felt the sadness of being left out or felt unwanted because of not having a date on Friday night or having to sit alone at lunch? Can you remember your first day at a new school? Remember how good it felt to find some familiar friends? Or how grateful you were when some new friends welcomed you?

God meant for us to live in communities. As a child, God places us into a family made up of those who live in our house (mom, dad, and siblings). We have larger, extended families (grandpa, grandma, aunts, uncles, cousins, and so forth). As we mature, we have our community families (church, school, clubs). Eventually, God intends most people to be joined with another for a lifetime as husband and wife. All these relationships are necessary. They provide different levels and types of support.

The need for others is part of what distinguishes men from God. We need God and we need each other. God needs no one, nothing else. That is why He is so well symbolized by the number one, while humans—and all creation—are reflected by the number two.

The symbolism of two is rooted in Adam and Eve. The first two people represent all people and all society. Without Eve, Adam was incomplete. God saw that it was not good that he was alone. Without Eve, Adam was missing more than his rib. It was not good when he was alone.

Adam needed Eve for more than warmth and physical aid, for more than a better reward or profit for his toil (Ecclesiastes 4:9). He needed her in order to be whole, to be complete.

At the close of each day of creating, the writer of Genesis says that God declares His creation "good." When God says, "It is not good that the man should be alone" (Genesis 2:18), He changes His pattern of declaring the creation "good." In Hebrew, the word *good* means more than just okay. It means true and right. Jesus says only God is good (Mark 10:18). For Adam to be *good* is for Adam to be as God intended him to be. Adam needed Eve for God to pronounce creation good, for him to be good. So, to this day, we are always part of another. Alone is not good. We are also defined by one another. For we are always somebody's son or daughter, somebody's student or employee, somebody's someone. We cannot be alone. We are not autonomous. We are contingent, always touching other parts of creation.

When we try to be alone, we get into trouble. We are selfish and indulgent in our depression and our anger. We commit our sins in secret. We keep them to ourselves and imagine ourselves somehow superior to other men. We separate ourselves and are absent from our brothers. Yet a man alone is vanity. A coal separated from the fire quickly grows cold.

All sins are committed against God (Psalm 51:4) but sins are also committed in some way against our neighbors. The human desire to be free of duty and relationship—to do what feels good and be autonomous—results from a desire to be like God. We become like Eve in the garden deciding she didn't need God's Word to guide her. She could see for herself that the fruit was "good for food, and that it was a delight to the eyes, and that the tree was to be desired to make one wise" (Genesis 3:6). The problem began with what she saw for herself. She tried to become *one*.

Read Matthew 19:4–6. Why does a man leave his father and mother?

A man leaves his father and mother to become joined to a wife. He cleaves to his wife because two is better than one and it is not good to be alone. However, one made from two—that is, husband and wife, a family—is made even better by adding One. The writer of Ecclesiastes reminds us a cord of three strands is not easily broken (4:12). Apart from this third—God—the two do not become one. Rather this man and this woman are one in the Lord, in the One who is one alone. God joins them together. In God they become one, one with another and one with Him.

Yet the preacher in Ecclesiastes means more than just husband and wife. For all who believe and trust in Christ are one in Him. Even without a husband or a wife, Jesus is forever the other, our second half. Without Him, as Adam without Eve, we are incomplete. Without Him, we are less than we were meant to be. It is not good for man to be alone so God joins Himself to us. He is the one who rewards our toil. He keeps us warm. He fights off our enemies (Ecclesiastes 4:9–11). Without Him, all is vanity. With Him, all is good and right. By His blood we have life; we will eat, drink, and be merry in His kingdom.

Two: Lives of Service

Read the section on Confession from Luther's Small Catechism. How does Luther urge us to examine ourselves? What difference does it make if we are a father, mother, son, or daughter? How does this relate to the number two?

God places each of us into this world in very specific relationships. They are neither accidental nor interchangeable. You are not merely a daughter. You are Jane's daughter. That specific place brings with it specific duties. Being Jane's daughter is different than being Mary's daughter, because Jane and Mary have different needs. Their daughters serve them differently.

Luther teaches us to examine ourselves in

the specific relationships God has given us. We do not examine ourselves against God in an abstract way. Rather God's Law finds its standard in our relationships to one another. We serve God by serving our neighbor. We sin against God when we sin against our neighbor. Our neighbor is not a hypothetical situation—he is real. He has a name. It is that of your mother, father, brother, sister, employer, and so on. Luther wants us to actually apply God's Law to our lives in the details because God cares about the details. He has placed each of us into these relationships on purpose, for our good and for the good of our neighbor.

As a Biblical symbol for man, the number two always has the idea of Adam and Eve behind it. Eve was given as a helper to Adam. She helps him; he helps her. Eve and her life defined Adam and his life and vice-versa. We are "one." We are always part of other people's lives and they are part of us. The number two indicates relationships and divisibility.

Read the Table of Duties from Luther's Small Catechism. This section lists a series of Bible passages. How is the number two reflected in each of them? How do they apply to you? What is the positive side of these "duties"?

The number two is implicit in these duties. All these duties are the proper service owed to others. There is nothing in this list about what we do for ourselves. It is all about living in relationships.

Some of the duties obviously apply to the students, "What hearers owe their pastors," " of citizens," "to children," "to youth," and "to everyone." But the other passages are just as applicable. When we know what our parents' duties are, we better understand our duties as children. But even more importantly, in learning what the duties of "bishops, pastors, and preachers" or even "widows" are, we learn how all God's people connect and are one body with many parts (Romans 12:1–21).

When we start to define ourselves in community and relationship, we begin to see our value in the world. God placed us in these offices, gives us these duties, with a purpose. We have work to do. These duties not only define sin, they also define good works. God uses us to preserve and sustain creation. He created these works for us to do (Ephesians 2:10).

In high school, most of our life is devoted to training. We are getting ready to be contributors to society and learning also how to be husbands and wives, sons and daughters. But it will not be too long before you are taking care of your parents. Already you serve them in more significant ways. When you were a small child, there was not much you could add to the household. Now you pitch in more and more with the chores. In this way, God provides for your parents and siblings even as God provided for you through them.

There is also a sense of being a recipient. These duties not only show us what to do, they also show us how God provides for us. Food doesn't fall out of the sky. It comes by means. For most of us that means Mom or Dad goes to work to earn money to buy food. Then someone takes that money to the store and buys it and brings it home. Then someone prepares and serves it. It is God who provides. He provides through these offices He has created for us. So we see in the duties not just the Law, but also a promise, a way that God operates in this world for our good.

Only God is one. We are never alone. We are forever two.

Creatures in Community

Read Genesis 6:11–22. How many of each animal did Noah take on the ark? Why do they come to Noah (verse 20)? Why male and female?

The animals come onto the ark in pairs, a male and a female of every living thing. (In the next chapter of Genesis, which we will read later, we will see Noah brings five more of some animals. He brings seven of the clean animals. But he brings at least two, one male and one female, of every species.)

The animals come to Noah so that he can keep them alive. Despite the fact that Noah's ark has been largely taken over in the popular imagination as a children's story, it is actually very violent. Noah's ark is a story filled with death and destruction. The flood was a judgment against man. Only one family of each species was spared. They were spared in order that the earth might be filled again, but that was it: one family, one "husband" and "wife" of each animal, no more. Humanity has the greatest representation. Noah's entire extended family, his sons and daughters-in-law along with his wife, were all spared. There were eight of them. In this number, there is a sense of fullness and special grace given to Noah. None of the animal families brought children. Noah's family has one more than the families of clean animals. This symbolizes that man is the ultimate creature, the true pinnacle of creation. There is also something in the number eight of the new day and new creation. But we will pick this up again in Lesson 6.

The animals who came to Noah weren't stuffed animals. They weren't cartoons. They were wild animals and included not only pairs of chipmunks, squirrels, and bunnies, but also scorpions, crocodiles, and poisonous snakes. Noah and his family not only had to work hard in building the ark while the world mocked them, they also had to work hard during their time in the ark to keep the animals alive and safe.

The whole thing is miraculous. It is miraculous that wild animals would hear the summons and come to Noah. It is miraculous that they would get into the ark. It is miraculous that they would not kill each other. It is even miraculous that they could all fit on the ark.

That being said, if God was going to perform so many miracles, why not just call the beasts from the earth again? Why not just make new animals after the flood receded? We can speculate, but the Bible doesn't say. What the Bible says is that God wasn't ready yet to destroy the world and rebuild it completely. He wanted it cleansed, but He hadn't given up on it. In order to cleanse it, he reduced it to its smallest element, and that element is two of each creature. What is true of man is also true of all creation. Even animals live in relationships and dependence upon others. Only God is one.

The world was cursed when Adam and Eve sinned in the garden. So also all the earth was punished when their sons and daughters turned from God at the time of Noah. The animals hadn't turned against God, but they were punished just the same. Even as mankind was reduced to a single family, so also was the animal kingdom. But even as all the earth was cursed, so also all the earth was redeemed when Jesus Christ died on the cross. The time has yet to come when this redemption will be fully delivered. Paul tells us that all of creation eagerly awaits Christ's return (Romans 8:18–23). All things—including heaven and earth—will pass away except the Word of God. There will be a new heaven and a new earth. Creation, including animals, will be restored to God's original, perfect, design (Isaiah 11:6–8; 65:25; Revelation 22:1–6).

Four

Read Genesis 2:10 and Revelation 7:1. Why four rivers and winds? Why the four "corners" of the earth when the earth is a globe, not a cube?

The simplest reproduction in mathematics is duplication. Man and wife are duplicated into son and daughter. Man and wife make two. Man, wife, son, and daughter make four. Certainly, a man and wife might have fewer children or no children. So also they might have many more than two. The number four is meant not as a literal number for the family but as a symbolic number. The idea is that the family is multiplying, reproducing. Each man and woman create more men and women. Hence the number four is a number of man and creation.

The earth itself also reflects the number four.

There are four seasons and four cardinal directions on a compass. The Bible refers to the "four winds" at least ten times (Jeremiah 49:36; Ezekiel 37:9; Daniel 7:2; 8:8; 11:4; Zechariah 2:6; 6:5; Matthew 24:31; Mark 13:27; and Revelation 7:1). The four rivers in Eden in Genesis 2 are described as watering the entire earth. They run to the very edges of the world. The four corners of the earth in Revelation 7 convey the idea that the angels are standing on the edge of the earth. All of the earth will be covered by the destructive winds they are holding back. In each case, the idea of four is meant to convey totality.

There are some other famous fours in the Bible: the four horseman of the Apocalypse in Revelation 6 and the four evangelists and Gospels—Matthew, Mark, Luke, and John. There are also some things Christian tradition has classified in fours for the sake of catechesis and memory: the four cardinal virtues (temperance, wisdom, patience, and justice); the four elements (earth, water, fire, and air); and the four last things (death, judgment, heaven, and hell).

Wings and the Creatures beneath Them

Read Revelation 4:6–14 again. There are a lot of details. Where do the numbers two and four come into play?

There are four living creatures that surround the throne where the One is seated. These creatures are covered with eyes. They see everything. Yet the only thing they see is the one on the throne. The Lamb of God is everything because He created all things. There is nothing besides Him. He always has been and will never cease to be.

These four living creatures are diligent and faithful in their service to Him. Each creature has six wings like the seraphim seen by Isaiah in his vision recorded in Isaiah 6. Wings also come in pairs. They are like arms and legs, feet and hands, eyes and ears. So they have three pairs of wings, three sets of two. The numbers two and four indicate balance.

Read Isaiah 6:1–3; Ezekiel 1:5–26; Ezekiel 10:3–22; and Revelation 4:6–8. Using the chart, write down how the similar creatures are described in each account. Are these the same creatures? Are they real or merely part of the vision? Why would we think they are real when we don't think the wheels in Ezekiel's vision are real? What is the symbolism of the four faces?

None of the visions calls the creatures angels. John calls them *living creatures* (Revelation 4:6) echoing Ezekiel 1:15. Commentator Horace Hummel makes the case that this is the best translation both in Ezekiel 1:15 and in Revelation 4:6 (*Concordia Commentary: Ezekiel 1–20*, p. 37–38) and that they are probably related. The winged creatures are named as *seraphim* in Isaiah 6:2 and as *cherubim* in Ezekiel 10:3.

> According to Ezekiel, the cherubim move in whatever direction the Spirit wills to go (Ezekiel 1:15–21; 10:9–22). Evidently whenever and wherever God moves, the cherubim move; hence the wheels within wheels in the vision enable the throne to move straight in any direction (Ezekiel 1:15–21). While in Ezekiel's vision the winged creatures move together with God and his throne, in the visions of both Isaiah and John, they seem to be positioned in one place, stationary with God's throne and presence. (*Concordia Commentary: Revelation*, p. 123)

Faces

John sees one *face* per creature. One has the face of a man, another of a lion, another of an ox, and the final one of an eagle (Revelation 4:7). Isaiah does not mention their faces. In Ezekiel's first vision of the creatures he sees the same faces as John, only he sees all four faces on each creature! Each creature had the face of a man, a lion, an ox, and an eagle (Ezekiel 1:10). In Ezekiel's second vision of these creatures, there is one change. Each creature still has four faces but this time the ox face has been replaced with a cherub (Ezekiel 10:14).

Wings

In all four visions, each creature has wings. In Isaiah (6:2) and Revelation (4:8), the winged creatures have six wings each, but in both of Ezekiel's visions they each have four wings (Ezekiel 1:11; 10:21). Isaiah reports that the seraphim all used one pair of wings to fly while one pair covered their feet and the other pair their faces (Isaiah 6:2). Ezekiel only reported four wings. He says that one pair was touching the wings of another creature and the other was used to cover their bodies (Ezekiel 1:11). John only tells us they have six wings, not what they are doing with them or why they need so many.

Eyes

John's creatures are full of eyes (Revelation 4:6). Isaiah does not mention eyes. Ezekiel's first vision doesn't mention eyes, but in the second vision he also says they were full of eyes (Ezekiel 10:12).

Voice

Both Isaiah and John hear the winged creatures singing. It is not the exact same hymn, but they both sing "Holy, Holy, Holy" (Isaiah 6:3; Revelation 4:8). Ezekiel does not hear singing. But he did hear a loud noise "like the sound of many waters" (Ezekiel 1:24) from the wings in the first vision.

Even though all of these passages are from visions and do not require a literal reading, the emphasis in Ezekiel and Revelation on these four beings as "living" creatures seems to indicate that they are real. It seems to make sense that these are real created beings, a special kind of angel, and that all four visions are describing the same creatures. Concerning the creatures in Revelation 4, Dr. Louis Brighton writes:

> In his vision of God's heavenly glory and throne, they [the winged creatures] are closer to God than any other creature, angelic or saintly. . . . whose glorious task is to lead the heavenly host in the praise and adoration of God. They could be thought of as the choir masters of the heavenly choir, whose joy and thanksgiving it is to sing the praises of their Lord and Creator. They initiate the worship (Revelation 4:9), and the saints and angels in heaven follow their lead (4:10–11; 5:11–12). (*Concordia Commentary: Revelation*, p. 126)

Even if these are real, literal angels, it may be that some of what the prophets and apostles saw regarding them was symbolic. The angel Michael is real and in John's vision he saw him carrying a chain. We understand that the chain was not literal but represented Michael's involvement in the defeat of Satan (Revelation 20:1–3). Thus it is possible that the reason they are all slightly different in the four accounts is due to what God wanted to convey through the symbolism of the vision.

All four visions indicate that there are four creatures. Ezekiel especially emphasizes the number four with the wheels and the four faces, and sides, of every creature. Dr. Brighton considers the symbolism of the four faces and the number four:

> Since these four winged creatures have different faces, which are likenesses from the animate part of God's creation, commentators throughout the Christian centuries have ascribed various symbolical meanings to the faces. Victorinus, the earliest Latin commentator (third century), says that the four creatures are *the four Gospels*. The lion is Mark; the man is Matthew; the ox is Luke; and the eagle is John. Irenaeus associated the four winged creatures with *four aspects of Christ's work*. The lion represents Christ's royal office, the ox his priestly office or character, the face of a man Christ's human nature, and the flying eagle the gift of the Spirit, which he gives to his church. According to Irenaeus, the four evangelists reflect these four characteristics of Christ's ministry. The eagle thus symbolizes Mark, the man Matthew, the ox Luke, and the lion John. Irenaeus also states that because there are four zones or directions of the earth and four winds, it is fitting that the church with the Gospel should have "four pillars," that is, a Gospel

with or under four aspects. Pseudo-Athanasius suggested that the man was Matthew, the ox Mark, the lion Luke, and the eagle John. Augustine has the lion as Matthew, the man as Mark, the ox as Luke, and the eagle as John. Oecumenius' Greek commentary on Revelation (sixth century) identified the four creatures with *the four elements*. The lion represents fire, the ox earth, the man air, and the eagle water. Another example of such symbolical interpretation is that of Honorius Augustodunensis, a twelfth-century scholastic hermit philosopher who probably lived near Regensburg. He suggested that the four winged creatures represented *the four stages in Christ's life*. The man represents the birth of Christ, the ox the death of Christ, the lion the resurrection, and the eagle the ascension of Christ.

While Scripture does not explicitly affirm those interpretations of the faces, there is biblical evidence that the *number* of the winged creatures is symbolic. Four suggests the totality of God's animate creation, "the four corners of the earth" (Revelation 7:1; 20:8). The man could represent the human race, the lion the animal kingdom, the ox domesticated animals, and the eagle the birds of the air. Yet ascribing such symbolic meanings does not deny the existence of these heavenly, angelic spirits; for, apart from any symbolism, they exist in their own right. *The winged creatures are, properly, representatives of God's total creation in worship before His heavenly throne* (see 5:13–14). The fact that they are full of eyes suggests that God in His 'ceaseless vigilance' oversees His creation as it is represented by the four winged creatures. The four would represent the entire creation of God as it was before the fall and/or as it will be when restored (see Romans 8:18–25; Revelation 21:1). The four could then also symbolize the four gospels because through the gospels the message of the Lord Christ is sent out into "the four corners of the earth" (7:1), and as a result of Christ's victory, all creation will be restored at the End. However the four creatures are interpreted, symbolically and/or as representatives, *they fulfill the godly role of attending God in his heavenly majesty*. In particular they lead the heavenly host, angelic and saintly, in singing the praises of God. (*Concordia Commentary: Revelation*, p. 126–127)

The creatures are weird. They are outside of our experience, unlike anything we've ever seen. Yet parts of them are familiar. One of the most familiar things about them is their number—four. In that number, we recognize that these creatures represent all of creation. They represent us. They cannot look straight into God's face, but they are not afraid. They are rejoicing in Him and worshiping Him. God is good and it is good to be in heaven. They also represent God's vigilance and care for us. There is nowhere He is not watching out over us, nor anyplace His holiness does not wash us clean, or His wings fail to cover us. Four creatures in heaven show us not only that all of creation worships Him, but also that He loves all of creation.

Conclusion

Once again we have seen how the Bible presents God's care for us. He provides for our needs in this life through our neighbors. He gives us good and valuable work to do for others. He gives our lives purpose in our neighbors. The details and the specifics of our lives matter to God. We have also seen how God's love covers the four corners of the earth. In the strange creatures around God's throne, gathered around the living Lamb who was slain, we see how heaven is waiting for us.

Closing Prayer

Isaiah, mighty seer in days of old,
The Lord of all in spirit did behold
High on a lofty throne, in splendor bright,
With robes that filled the temple courts
with light.
Above the throne were flaming seraphim;
Six wings had they, these messengers
of Him.
With two they veiled their faces as
was right,
With two they humbly hid their feet
from sight,
And with the other two aloft they soared;
One to the other called and praised
the Lord:
"Holy is God, the Lord of Sabaoth!
Holy is God, the Lord of Sabaoth!
Holy is God, the Lord of Sabaoth!
His glory fills the heavens and the earth!"
The beams and lintels trembled at
the cry,
And clouds of smoke enwrapped the
throne on high. Amen.

("Isaiah Mighty Seer in Days of Old," *LSB* 960)

TWO AND FOUR: CREATION COUNTED

Man is Never One, Never Alone

Read **Ecclesiastes 4:7–12**. What is the "vanity" that the author is writing about? What solution does he offer? Read **Genesis 2:18–25**. What is not good? Compare this text to the verses from Ecclesiastes.

Read **Proverbs 17:17** and **Proverbs 18:24**. How do these verses reinforce this theme?

Read **Matthew 19:4–6**. Why does a man leave his father and mother?

Two: Lives of Service

Read the section on Confession from Luther's Small Catechism. How does Luther urge us to examine ourselves? What difference does it make if we are a father, mother, son, or daughter? How does this relate to the number two?

Read the Table of Duties from Luther's Small Catechism. This section lists a series of Bible passages. How is the number two reflected in each of them? How do they apply to you? What is the positive side of these "duties"?

Creatures in Community

Read **Genesis 6:11–22**. How many of each animal did Noah take on the ark? Why do they come to Noah **(v. 20)**? Why male and female?

Four

Read these passages:

A river flowed out of Eden to water the garden, and there it divided and became four rivers. **Genesis 2:10**

After this I saw four angels standing at the four corners of the earth, holding back the four winds of the earth, that no wind might blow on earth or sea or against any tree. **Revelation 7:1**

Why four rivers and winds? Why the four "corners" of the earth when the earth is a globe, not a cube?

Wings and the Creatures beneath Them

Read **Revelation 4:6–14** again. There are a lot of details. Where do the numbers two and four come into play?

Read **Isaiah 6:1–3**; **Ezekiel 1:5–26**; **Ezekiel 10:3–22**; and **Revelation 4:6–8**. Using the chart, write down how the similar creatures are described in each account. Are these the same creatures? Are they real or merely part of the vision? Why would we think they are real when we don't think the wheels in Ezekiel's vision are real? What is the symbolism of the four faces?

Isaiah 6:1–3 Seraphim	**Ezekiel 1:5–26** Living Creatures	**Ezekiel 10:3–22** Cherubim	**Revelation 4:6–8** Living Creatures

4

Five and Ten: Keys to God's Word

Lesson Focus

The next three lessons are all numbers that are built on the numbers in the first three lessons (one, two, three, and four). This lesson will take up the numbers five and ten. Though not exclusively so, five and ten are particularly numbers of the Law. The Law shows us what God expects of us or what we should do. Because we do not always do what we should, because we never have pure and perfect motives, the Law shows us our sin and our need for God's saving grace in Christ Jesus. We will see how God uses five and ten in the Bible to demonstrate our need and His solution for us in Jesus Christ.

Opening Prayer

Blessed Father in heaven, You are abundant in goodness and truth, forgiving iniquity, transgression, and sin. I thank You for the grace and mercy assured me by the redemption of Your Son. In Your fatherly love look down on Your disloyal child. "Cast me not away from Thy presence, and take not Thy Holy Spirit from me. Restore to me the joy of Thy salvation, and uphold me with a willing Spirit." Have mercy on me for Christ's sake, and forgive what I have done wrong and what I have left undone. Quiet my troubled conscience with the knowledge of sins forgiven. By faith in Christ fill my heart with the joy of adoption into the family of heaven. Engraft me as a living branch upon Your Son, the Vine, that I may bring forth fruit in abundance by leading a holy and blameless life to the glory of Your name and for the benefit of all people. Help me ever to live in Your favor and finally to die in Your peace; for the sake of Jesus Christ, my Lord and Redeemer. Amen.

(*My Prayer Book*, p.65)

Five

Symbolism can be found in a number's factors or by addition. In the first lesson, we studied Jesus admonishing Peter to forgive his brother seven times seventy. Adding or multiplying numbers always gives them a sense of fullness. Five and ten are made of the numbers two and three (5=2+3; 10=5X2).

List the first five books of the Bible. Who wrote them? What is the significance of the number five?

Moses wrote the first five books of the Bible. They are: Genesis, Exodus, Leviticus, Numbers, and Deuteronomy. In Hebrew they are called the *Torah,* the Law. This was the most important part of the Old Testament, perhaps the most important portion of the entire Bible, for the children of Israel. Everything we know and believe about God and our life in Him is found in the Book of Genesis. Some of it is not fully developed. God follows this revelation to Moses with further details and fuller revelation. But all our doctrine is there—creation, redemption, and sanctification. Genesis does not only contain the story of creation and the fall. It also proclaims the promise of the Messiah, the making of a people by grace out of nothing. It takes us from our first parents all the way through Joseph's reign in Egypt. When we add Exodus to Genesis, we get the birth of the nation Israel when God delivers the people out of bondage. We also hear the personal name of God, YHWH, for the first time. (See Lesson 2.)

Leviticus, Numbers, and Deuteronomy add the Ten Commandments and the ceremonial laws that foreshowed the Messianic sacrifice and redemption to come. What is true for Genesis is true for all of the five books of Moses. The rest of the Bible simply fills in the details and comments upon what Moses wrote. Moses doesn't give us everything we know. He doesn't give us the place of the Messiah's birth or what His human name will be. He doesn't give us the details of His betrayal and crucifixion. But nothing new is added to what Moses wrote. Because of this, the number five came to be associated with the fullness of God's self-revelation or God's Word. Once again we find the symbolism of a number is rooted in the real history of God's people.

Next to the idea of God's Word, five is also important because it is a compound number. It is the number of man (2) plus the number of God (3) or the numbers of creation (4) and God (1). Both ways of adding end up with the same result. The idea is that five is a number greater than man, or it is the number of man and his duties, or of man and God, or of creation and the Creator. Five is also a prime number. It has no factors. It is not divisible except by itself and one. Prime numbers have special status. They are indivisible, solid, and full.

There are at least two other places in the Bible where we might see the idea of man and God coming together in God's Word. In John's Gospel, we read, "the Word became flesh and dwelt among us, and we have seen His glory, glory as of the only Son from the Father, full of grace and truth" (John 1:14). The only Son from the Father is true God and also true man. He became flesh. He is also God's Word. God called His creation into being by this Word (John 1:3). He meets His creation by this same Word. This Word, our Lord Jesus Christ, is expressed and revealed in the Scriptures. Even though we don't see the number five in John 1:14, we see the idea of God joining Himself to men by the Word (2 + 3). We see this same concept in 2 Peter 1:21, "For no prophecy was ever produced by the will of man, but men spoke from God as they were carried along by the Holy Spirit." The Scriptures are God's self-revelation for men, but men wrote them. Even though we don't have the number five named, we see that what the Bible says about itself resonates with the symbolism of five—God joins Himself to man in His Word.

These two things, the number of the books of Moses and the idea of God's Word and the mathematical circumstances (2+3 and prime) invest five with meaning. Both of these ideas convey completion or totality and point us to the fulfillment of Jesus Christ.

Read the following passages: Matthew 5:17; 7:12; 11:13; Luke 24:44; John 1:45; Acts 28:23; and Romans 3:21. What is meant by the "Law and the Prophets"? What is the Law? Who are the Prophets? How is this connected to the five books of Moses? What numbers are added to get five?

The phrase "the Law and the Prophets" or "Moses and the Prophets" refers to the Old Testament. The Hebrews divided the Old Testament into three sections: the Law, or the five books of Moses; the Psalms; and the Prophets, which included everything else in our Old Testament. Since the New Testament had not been written at the time of the Old Testament, the Law and the Prophets was shorthand for the Bible or God's revealed Word and will. Sometimes this was even shortened further to simply *the Law*. As we discussed in Lesson 2, when the word *Law* is used this way, it doesn't mean just the demands and expectations of God but also includes the Good News of God's love in the Messiah. In fact, Moses wrote more about the Messiah than Matthew, Mark, Luke, or John did!

Read Genesis 3:15. This passage is in the Law section of Scripture. Is it Law or Gospel? Who is it about? Who is Eve's first son? How is five implied? Read also Colossians 1:13–20.

This passage falls within the Torah, the law written by Moses, but this passage is a promise from God to send His offspring through Eve to crush the tempter's head. It is the Gospel in the narrow sense, for it "shows us our Savior and the grace of God" (Small Catechism). Sometimes this passage has been called the *first Gospel*. It immediately follows the fall of Adam and Eve into sin. God speaks these words to the serpent before He pronounces the Law's judgment and curse upon Adam and Eve. Following this passage, Adam first calls his mate *Eve*. For Eve is "the mother of all living" (Genesis 3:20). By her offspring, all men will be saved. Even though she is not the direct mother of the Messiah, she is the first woman, and what is promised here to Eve is fulfilled in Mary, and also to us.

Cain was the first son born to Eve (Genesis 4:1) but Genesis 3:15 promises an older Son. In Colossians 1:15, Paul calls Jesus Christ the first-born of all creation. He is the seed of Eve come to reconcile us to Himself by the blood of His cross. God joins Himself to Mary as the fulfillment of the promise. As God and Man joined together and the very Word of God (John 1), He is the ultimate five.

Read God's instructions to Moses about the altar in Exodus 27:1–2. Why five cubits by five cubits? And why three high? What is the shape of the altar in your church? Does it have any decorations on the top of it? How many wounds did Jesus have?

The word *altar* in Hebrew is a derivative of the word for sacrifice. An altar was a place of sacrifice. It was a place where animals were killed for sins they did not commit.

The Bible does not say why the top of the altar was supposed to be a square, five cubits by five cubits. Some scholars have suggested that the five by five altar reminds us of the Ten Commandments and of the five books of Moses. It was a symbol of God's Word, containing both demands and promises. If it had been four cubits by four cubits, it might well have reminded them of the four corners of the earth, but it wasn't. It was five. It was man's number joined to God's number (2+3). Details are not accidental. God cares about the details.

That altar might have been almost any height, but it wasn't. It was three cubits high. Again, some scholars have suggested that this number reminds us that God Himself, that most Holy Trinity, would be present on this altar. The "horns" of the altar were like pointy bumps on the corners. The altar was not flat. It sloped upwards at the corners. It was somewhat concave in the middle. These "horns" probably helped to hold the sacrifices in place. At the very least, they made it less likely that a sacrifice would roll off.

Since we no longer sacrifice animals in the church today, our altars are not built to hold the blood and bodies of sacrificial animals. They don't need horns to keep things in place. Today's altars symbolize our Lord's sacrifice on the cross. Today's altar serves as a table where Christ serves us His Supper, His body and blood. The corners and sides of our altars are the same height as the middle, so they are flat. Even though no blood is ever spilled on them, we still call them *altars*, and we still call the corners of our altars *horns*. Your pastor knows this and you can find it in liturgical books. This vocabulary, *altar* and *horns*, is a deliberate attempt to tie our worship to the worship instituted by God in the Old Testament.

At one time, God required blood sacrifices to foreshow the death of the Messiah. Now the Messiah has been sacrificed. The promise has not changed; the heart of our religion is still the sacrifice of the Messiah. God came to His people of old by blood. He comes now by blood as well. He came then by the blood of animals as an example of something innocent dying for the guilty. Now He comes in the blood of Jesus Christ, raised from the dead, given to believers to drink for the forgiveness of sins.

Despite the instructions given for the tabernacle altar in Exodus, our altars are not typically square. The altars in our churches don't typically look like the altar described in Exodus. Most church altars are rectangular. That is to make them into the shape of a coffin as well as a table. Instead of horns sticking up to hold the sacrifice in place and the sides being five cubits long, traditional church altars have five crosses on them. They have a cross carved into each corner and a cross in the middle of the top. Ask your altar guild or pastor if your altar has those crosses. Those little crosses, which usually look like plus symbols, are reminders of the five wounds our

Lord suffered on the cross. The five wounds were from the nails in His hands and feet and from the centurion's spear into His side. The number helps tie Jesus' death to the five books of Moses and the Law.

No matter the shape of the altar in your church, the sacrifice remains the same—the body and blood of Jesus given and shed for the remission of sins and the proclamation of His atoning death and His glorious resurrection. It is what Moses and Abraham confessed. It is what they waited for. There are no more sacrifices to be offered. God has joined Himself to men to make us free.

Read John 20:24–29. How does Jesus convince Thomas that it is really Him? If you were trying to convince someone of your identity, how would you do it? How does that relate to Christian altars with five crosses carved on them? How does the number of Jesus' wounds relate to the books of Moses?

The Bible does not describe Jesus looking into Thomas' eyes. That is the kind of thing we might do to convince someone we were telling the truth or that it was really us. It is usually the first way we recognize someone. Nor did Jesus remind Thomas of something they did together or of something only He would know about Thomas. Instead He invited Thomas to look at the marks left by the nails in His hands and the place where the spear was thrust. Jesus said: "Put your finger here, and see My hands; and put out your hand, and place it in My side. Do not disbelieve, but believe" (John 20:27). The marks on Jesus' body convinced Thomas that it was really Jesus.

Some Christians connect Jesus bearing five marks from the cross as a reminder of the five books of Moses. Everything Moses foretold is fulfilled in the death and resurrection of Jesus Christ. The number five reminds us of God's Word and God's Word has come true in Jesus. Moses gave us the Law that put Jesus to death. That Law now has nothing more to say. Moses always told us God's promise of the coming Savior. Thomas recognized the Savior by those five marks.

Read Revelation 5:6. What does "as though it had been slain" mean? Do you think anyone else in heaven looks "as though he had been slain"?

Even though Jesus is raised from the dead and His body is perfected, He still bears marks from His wounds. The wounds have healed, but He still bears the marks of how He died. Those marks are the badge of His office. By dying for us, He fulfilled His Father's will. Because Jesus laid down His life for us, His Father loves Him and His Father loves us. It is possible that our Lord could have had other scars. He might have fallen out of a tree as a boy or suffered some accident in his stepfather's shop. But those scars don't matter like the five left by the cross. John sees Jesus in heaven like a living Lamb that had been slain. He was slain but He lives. The Law of Moses—all five books—is complete.

The Bible describes the saints in heaven as dressed in white (Revelation 7:9–14). When our bodies are raised and perfected, they will be uncorrupted, glorious, powerful, and spiritual (1 Corinthians 15:42–44).

Read the following passages: Psalms 41:13; 72:18–19; 89:52; 106:48; and 150:1–6. What do the passages have in common? Why would we bless the Lord? What is different about the fifth passage?

Each of the passages is the last verse of a psalm. All of the verses quoted, except the verse from Psalm 150, contain the phrase: "Blessed be the Lord." The biblical book we call *Psalms* is really a collection of psalms. Various human authors wrote the psalms over a long period of time. The Book of Psalms is similar to a modern-day hymnal. When the psalms were first collected and put together on a single scroll, they were organized into five little chapters or books. Each of the verses you just read is at the end of a book of psalms. The books are Psalms 1–41, 42–72, 73–89, 90–106, and 107–150. Some of the books of psalms seem to be thematically related, but the divisions are mostly arbitrary. Despite the fact that the divisions were somewhat arbitrary, the number of the divisions was not. The psalms were organized into five "books" in order to mirror the books of Moses and pay homage to the number five. As Moses gave the people five books of the Law, David was giving the people five hymnals of praise and thanksgiving.

What does the word *bless* mean? Why do we say in the liturgy "Let us bless the Lord"? How can we bless the Lord? What does the word *alleluia* mean?

We usually think of the word *bless* as belonging to God. It is what He does, not what we do. We use the word *bless* to describe God giving or doing something nice. We say God has blessed someone who has a nice car or a good singing voice. We say, "God bless you," to someone as a prayer. We are asking God to do something nice for the person. We use the word sarcastically when we say something like, "She blessed us with her presence," to mean that she is snotty and arrogant and thought she was doing us a favor simply by being around us.

Certainly the word *bless* is correctly used to talk about what God does for men. But that is the problem. That is not quite what the Hebrew word means.

Our common use of the word *bless* usually refers to endowing favor upon someone. But the Hebrew word *barak* would best be defined as "to praise or glorify." Because of this distinction in meaning between the English *bless* and the Hebrew *barak,* I think we might be better off with a transliteration instead of a translation.

To translate a word is to give its meaning in another language. Some words are not translated; they are transliterated. That means they are brought into another language with the same sounds as the original but with the letters from the new language. The words "Christ" (*christos* in Greek = anointed one) and "Messiah" (*meshiach* in Hebrew = anointed one) are transliterated into English. They could be translated. We know that they mean anointed one. But that translation is shallow compared to either of the words "Christ" or "Messiah." So we stick with an English version of the original.

The Hebrew word that is translated as "bless" would be pronounced in English something like "barak." It means to pronounce good things. In the Greek Old Testament, it is translated with the word *eulogeo.* That word is transliterated into English as "eulogy." It is made up of two words in Greek. The Greek word *eulogeo* that translates the Hebrew word *barak* means "good words." In English we use the word *eulogy* to describe a speech at a funeral where good words are said about a dead person. But that is not the way the words *eulogeo* or *barak* are translated. They are translated with the same English word—*bless.* That translation isn't wrong. It is just insufficient. If the word *bless* carries the normal idea of doing something nice, it doesn't make much sense for us to bless God, but if the word means "nice words" or "to say nice things about," then it does.

When we realize that God does nice things for us—blesses us—by speaking—by good words, we open up something of God's character. When God said, "Let there be light," there was. God spoke it into being. When God speaks good things about us they happen. So when He blesses us, when He says good words, it actually does something. God works through words. It is the Word that became flesh and dwelt among us. When we speak good things about God it doesn't do anything, but we are telling the truth. It doesn't change things, but it pleases God. It is praise. Our blessing of the Lord is not doing something for Him but rather telling who He is. He is the one who is good.

Thus each of the first four books of Psalms end with a little exclamation of praise. Bless the Lord is, "Say good things about God." This device is used not only to remind us to tell the truth about God, but also to draw attention to the structure of the book, to emphasize the fivefold character of the Psalms. Why? Because matching the structure of the books of Moses and taking up the number of God plus the number of man (3+2) meant that the Book of Psalms was full and trustworthy. The book could have been divided differently or with a different ascription of praise. This choice was very deliberate. Saying good things about God (bless) is the Mosaic way (five). It is also the way that God (three) has given us (two) to speak of Him. Notice that "LORD" is in all caps in each of these verses. This is not just any God. This is the God who spoke to Moses from the burning bush.

The fifth book, as the capstone to the entire collection, is an entire psalm of praise. It uses the more celebratory word for praise in Hebrew—*Alleluia*. *Alleluia* is made of two Hebrew words. The first word means "praise or glorify." You can hear the second word at the end. It is the personal name of God—Yahweh. Again, it could be translated, "Praise the Lord." But if it were it would lose something.

Read Leviticus 14:1–32. Why were lepers treated this way? Why was the ceremony to be declared "clean" so complicated and drawn-out? Do you remember the distinction about the types of laws in the Old Testament?

To our modern sensibilities, the treatment of lepers doesn't seem fair. It was, however, part of the Old Testament ceremonial law. The fear of infectious disease for which there was no cure was a reality to the people of the biblical age. God had established these laws to protect His people from the spread of disease.

There were three types of laws in the Old Testament: moral, civil, and ceremonial. The first type of law is the moral law, "which tells all people their duty toward God and other people" (*Small Catechism*, p. 55). These Old Testament laws are still binding. They show us the difference between right and wrong. The penalties for stealing are determined by the civil law, but the fact that stealing is wrong and is a sin against God is established and confessed by the moral law. The moral law is contained most fully in the Ten Commandments, but is summarized most succinctly by our Lord, "You shall love the Lord your God with all your heart and with all your soul and with all your mind. This is the great and first commandment. And a second is like it: You shall love your neighbor as yourself. On these two commandments depend all the Law and the Prophets" (Matthew 22:37–40).

The second type of law is civil law. Old Testament civil laws are the political laws that governed the nation. For example, we read in Exodus 22:1, "If a man steals an ox or a sheep, and kills it or sells it, he shall repay five oxen for an ox, and four sheep for a sheep." While stealing ox or sheep and killing or selling them is still wrong, the penalty for such crimes is set by our government and not by this passage. If one of us steals an oxen or a sheep in the United States, he will not be accountable according to this passage but according to the criminal code of American law. A modern example is any law against stealing.

Since God has appointed a government (Romans 13:1) for our good, the civil laws of this government are binding for us. If we violate those laws, we break the Fourth Commandment. There is an exception, of course. We are to obey God rather than men (Acts 5:29). We obey God rather than men only if what men are asking us to do violates God's moral law.

The final type of law in the Old Testament is ceremonial law. Ceremonial laws governed the worship and diet of God's people. They were told exactly how and when and where to do or not do certain things. Some of these laws seemed to serve no real purpose except to set the Israelites apart from the other nations, to make them distinct, and to be a reminder to them of the discipline and grace under which they lived. Chief among these are the dietary regulations that were lifted with the ascension of Jesus Christ

(Acts 10:9–16). Most interesting, though, are the laws that described in painstaking detail the construction of the tabernacle and temple and the sacrifices that were necessary.

The ceremonial laws, whether they were instructions for worship or diet, are not binding on us today because the sacrifice of Jesus Christ is complete. The new Temple is the one built without hands, raised again and rebuilt by the Father on the third day. Unlike the civil laws, we have no modern equivalent. We do not have to follow them in any way. Yet they are very instructive for us. They show us who God is for us in the Messiah.

The laws regarding lepers were part of the ceremonial law. Part of the reason they were declared unclean is that their disease was the result of sin in the world. Their disease was a particularly apt symbol for sin since it was so infectious (Leviticus 13:1–46). In the same way, women were ceremonially unclean for forty days after giving birth (Leviticus 12:1–4) and anyone who touched a dead body was unclean for seven days (Numbers 19:16). Women were unclean after childbirth because the pain and blood of childbirth came as a part of the curse (Genesis 3:16). It wasn't supposed to be this way. Pain and sorrow were multiplied in childbirth because of sin. This is also true of death. We were not meant to die but, because Adam and Eve ate the forbidden fruit, we all die (Genesis 2:17). We cannot escape it. At some point, all of us will have to face the death of a loved one and deal with the body—but it should not be so. We were not created to die and would not die except for sin in the world (Romans 5:12). The people of Israel were kept constantly aware of these things through the ceremonial law. That is not to say that the lepers were cursed in particular because of their own personal sins. Rather the whole sad affair was a witness to the brokenness of creation because of sin. Even today, we are often afflicted by death in unfair and impersonal ways. The ceremonial law wasn't fair. It wasn't nice. It was harsh, seemingly arbitrary, and bloody.

Leprosy is an especially good symbol of sin; it was deadly, visible, and thought to be very contagious. The ceremonies involved not only cleansing or forgiving the leper but also bringing a healed leper back into the fold. Leprosy had separated him from his people. The ritual restored him in body, soul, and community. The rituals were complicated and drawn-out to illustrate the severe problem of sin in our lives and how it separates us from God and each other and to show how much it has cost God to restore us. The ritual helps to show us the great effort God has made on our behalf in Jesus Christ. It is no small thing that the burdens of the ceremonial laws have been lifted from us. The death and resurrection of Jesus Christ took those burdens and accusations from us (Paul calls the Old Testament Law a "yoke" in Acts 15:10). Jesus changed Old Testament worship from something that we had to do to a picture of who God is for us, even as He changed death to life.

Look again at Leviticus 14:14, 25. What are the differences? What is the significance of marking the leper in these ways? Why put oil on top of the blood? What does the word *anoint* mean? When was Jesus anointed? When were you anointed?

Verse 14 describes the healed leper who could afford a greater sacrifice, while verse 25 describes the ceremony for a poor person. The reality was that most lepers were poor beggars.

In putting blood from the animal to be sacrificed on the healed leper, the priest was anointing him. He was marking him as the one for whom the animal would be sacrificed. The animal's innocent blood was placed on the healed leper to make him innocent by covering his sins. Meanwhile, his guilt was placed upon the animal. Moses wrote that this was the atonement of the healed leper. The sacrifice and ceremony cleansed him. So also during the last plague in Egypt, the tenth plague, the blood of a sacrificed lamb was placed onto the doorposts of the believers' homes. When the angel of death came, he took the firstborn sons of all the households, even of the cattle, but he "passed over" the homes marked with blood. They were spared. The lamb died instead of the son (Exodus 12:13).

The word *atonement* is always used in the Book of Leviticus in connection with sacrifices (fifty-one times in forty-five verses). It always means that God has been appeased and satisfied. Animals were never sacrificed by God's people as a gift to God, as though God were hungry in some way or would enjoy these animals. They were never given simply in thanksgiving. They were always given as a substitute, as the innocent for the guilty. That is why Moses writes that the man has been cleansed. He had already been healed of leprosy. The sacrifice was not medicinal. It placed the innocent blood on a guilty man, on a sinner, so that his soul would be as clean as his skin. His sins were forgiven.

There is some significance also to the marking itself. The word *anoint* means "to mark." The Hebrew word for *anoint* is transliterated into English as *Messiah*. The Hebrew word *Messiah* is translated into Greek as *christos*, which is transliterated into English as *Christ*. When we say "Jesus Christ" we are really saying "Jesus the Messiah," which is really saying "Jesus the Anointed One." Anointing was how kings were marked in the Old Testament. They were marked and set aside from the rest of the people to be king.

But the Anointed One is the one anointed by God as the sacrifice for the sins of the world. The kings were only types of Him. The lepers were anointed to join them to the One who would die for them. To be anointed was to be "messiah-ed." They were little christs, little anointed ones, by the blood of an innocent animal that represented the human blood that Jesus would shed to forgive their sins and make them not only ceremonially or physically clean but also spiritually clean. They were marked with blood and oil on their head, hands, and feet to show that their whole bodies were cleansed and redeemed.

The Father anointed Jesus with the Holy Spirit when He was baptized by John in the Jordan River. That is why Jesus began His public ministry after His Baptism. That was the moment that marked or anointed Him as the Messiah. Even though we don't follow the ceremonial laws of the Old Testament, we do have anointings. You were anointed with water and the Holy Spirit when you were baptized into the name of the Father, the Son, and the Holy Spirit. Like a cleansed leper, you were christened, anointed, marked, messiah-ed. That is to say, you were joined to the death and resurrection of Jesus Christ, faith was born, and your sins were forgiven.

Ten

Read Luke 17:11–19. How many lepers are involved in this account? How does this relate to Leviticus 14? Why does the Samaritan return? How does this relate to the Law?

When Jesus sends the ten lepers to go see the priests, He is telling them to get started on the ritual cleaning and sacrifice outlined in Leviticus 14. Some scholars have suggested that it is not an accident that Jesus met ten lepers. Ten is five doubled. They represent all of man, for if a man is head, arms, and legs, five things, and man is two, always in relationship to another, then five plus five, or ten, is symbolic of all humanity while also calling to mind the Ten Commandments.

The ten lepers cried out to Jesus for mercy. He was merciful to them and sent them on their way. As they went, they were cleansed. The Greek New Testament uses the same word for *cleansed* in verse 14 as the Greek Old Testament in Leviticus 14:18, 19, and 20. What took two weeks, was costly, smelly, and cumbersome and was hidden in types and shadows in the Old Testament was accomplished by a simple word from Jesus. They did not need to undergo the temple ritual to be cleansed. They were healed and cleansed by a single word from Jesus. The mercy for which they prayed, He gladly gave. But only one leper recognized this.

The one who recognized this was a Samaritan. He had nowhere to go anyway. He could not go to the temple. The other nine could be ritually cleansed and restored to the congregation Israel. But this man was unclean also in his person. There was no Old Testament ritual to make a Gentile a Jew. He could be circumcised. He could belong. But he would always be an outsider. So he turns to Jesus and receives more than a mere healing. He receives salvation. With a word, he is transformed into the new Israel—God's own child. He was made whole.

Why not the others? If they were cleansed, why did Jesus send them to the priests? The hour of fulfillment had not yet come. It was fitting for them to fulfill the Law. That is not to say that they could not have turned to Jesus also. They should have recognized Jesus was YHWH, present to save them. Jesus' rhetorical question to the Samaritan clearly shows His disappointment (Luke 11:17–18). Even if they did not have another chance to see Jesus in the temple sacrifices, the old Law was being completed. Until Jesus pronounced "It is finished" (John 19:30) from the cross, the ceremonial law was still binding. That is why sacrifices were made for Jesus when He was presented at the temple (Luke 2:24).

Read the Ten Commandments in Exodus 34:27–29. How many commandments are there?

Read Exodus 20:1–17. Number the commandments from the Bible. How many are there? Compare that numbering to the numbering in the Small Catechism. Are there any repetitions in the Commandments?

In Exodus 34:28, it clearly states that there are Ten Commandments. This is also stated in Deuteronomy 4:13 and 10:4. The Ten Commandments themselves are given twice in the Bible, once in Exodus 20:3–17 and once in Deuteronomy 5:7–21. The Commandments are not numbered either time they are given. Neither text even says there are Ten Commandments. The Bible does not say, "The First Commandment is you shall have no other gods before Me." It simply states the Commandments without either numbering them or counting them. They are counted in Exodus 34:28 and also in Deuteronomy 4:13 and 10:4. When we try to count them in Exodus 20 or Deuteronomy 5, it seems to break down. It appears as though there are only nine.

The Early Church solved this problem by dividing the last commandment (Exodus 20:17) so that we have two commandments (nine and ten) against coveting. At the time of the Church's Reformation, Martin Luther and the other reformers followed this tradition since it contained no false doctrine. John Calvin was a reformer in Geneva who was a little younger and a little later than Luther. His teachings are the main influence on the majority of non-Lutheran Protestant churches. Calvin went further than Luther did on many things, thinking Luther was still too Catholic. Calvin was unsatisfied with dividing the last commandment, so he divided the First Commandment. Instead of two commandments on coveting he has two commandments on having no other gods. That is why the numbering of Protestant commandments is different than the Lutheran and Catholic numbering.

No matter how the dilemma is solved, there seems to be a numbering problem. The number ten seems more symbolic than literal. The counting just doesn't add up. Besides our inability to count these commandments so that they come to ten in a fully satisfactory way, Jesus reduces the commandments to simply two, love God and love neighbor (Luke 10:27). This should be a good indicator to us that the number ten is symbolic. To say there are Ten Commandments is to say the Law is complete. It covers every aspect of our lives.

There is, however, another possible solution, one that apparently never occurred to either Luther or Calvin. The first commandment is no commandment, or at least, it is not a commandment in the narrow sense. It is a promise.

Instead of starting our count at verse 3 with the first demand God makes, "you shall have no other gods," we can start counting at verse 2, "I am the LORD your God, who brought you out of the land of Egypt, out of the house of slavery" (Exodus 20:2). This follows the pattern in Genesis 3 where God first promises the sending of the Savior and restoration of Adam and Eve before He pronounces the curse (Genesis 3:15–19). It also seems to be echoed in Jesus' summary of the Law in Mark 12. When Jesus was asked, "Which commandment is the most important of all?" He answered, "The most important is, 'Hear, O Israel: The LORD our God, the Lord is one'" (Mark 12:29). Then He continued with the same summary He gave elsewhere: "'And you shall love the Lord your God with all your heart and with all your soul and with all your mind and with all your strength.' The second is this: 'You shall love your neighbor as yourself.' There is no other commandment greater than these" (Mark 12:30–31).

The Law's Purpose

Whatever the solution to the counting is, the Bible is clear that there are Ten Commandments in the Holy Law of God. There are ten rules for life that we fail to keep. Their simplicity is as sharp as polished steel. There is no denying or resisting it. It cuts to expose our cancerous souls. We are not good. We are not right. We are not healthy. Ten Commandments, ten rules for life, ten guides for our behavior, ten policies of self-control and decency, ten obviously correct ideals that we know we should be, all of which, without fail, we fail to keep. Ten little lines, a full and perfect Law, one for each leper who was healed.

We are quick to point out that erring is human. But are the Commandments really that hard? Honor your father and mother? We can do that. At least, we should be able to. It is not really asking much. Love your wife? That makes sense as well. So does "Tell the truth." These commandments are all good. They not only tell us what God wants, they are also what we want. Even the first table of the Law—believing in God—is not that hard. We agree that we should. These rules are not unreasonable. They are not unobtainable. They should not seem impossible. At our best, we do all of these, in part, part of the time. Why not always? Why not fully? The brutal Law leaves no escape. There is no excuse. We have failed to keep the Law in even a single point, for even a single day.

We have reasons and excuses. We are weak. We are sinful. We live in the inheritance of the first and fallen Adam. We were born this way! But there is no real excuse, no justification for our selfishness and hurtful indulgences. There is nothing, no extenuating circumstances, no once-in-a-lifetime event that makes our lies, violence, lust, and greed okay. It is just wrong. And confessing that, God's goodness and truth and our failure and sin, is the beginning of faith. The truth of the Law must have its way. It must cut off every retreat, every escape, every excuse. It must force us to our knees, to confession, to death. We must fall upon Christ and be broken by the Law lest He fall on us and we be crushed to powder (Matthew 21:44). We have Ten Commandments, all of which we have failed to keep. We thus deserve to die eternally. That would be the fair and just thing.

Our plea to heaven then cannot be for justice, for equity, or for fair treatment by the Law. That would simply be asking for hell. Like that of the lepers, our prayer must be a plea for mercy, for undeserved pardon, for redemption with someone else's blood. Let us learn from the lepers who stood far off and cried to God in the flesh for mercy. They hoped for mercy from the Son of Mary adopted by Joseph, who would be nailed to the cross for blasphemy He did not commit and who would raise Himself up again. They looked to Him for mercy and they got it! All ten got it. All ten were healed and cleansed, whether they were good or bad, whether they meant their prayer or not, they all got mercy. He died for everyone and was ready to accept every one of them back into His arms. Ten, remember, is the symbolic number not just of the Commandments, but also of humanity. The full Law, every bit of it, has been filled, completed, finished in Christ. All Ten Commandments and the sum total of humanity, every man, woman, or child ever to live, or who ever will live was redeemed and purchased on the cross of Jesus Christ. He died for the sins of the whole world and declared the entire human race to be reconciled to the Father. Only one leper, however, knew it. Only one returned to give thanks.

That is what faith does. It prays, praises, and thanks God. It comes back for more mercy. It comes to bask in the gracious and forgiving love of God. He did not come to give Jesus something, to bring His offering envelope or His praise. He did not come to feed Jesus or to learn how to be a healer for others. He came back to get something, to be fed, to be nourished, to be healed some more. That is what worship is. It is what faith does. Jesus needs nothing from us. We need everything from Him. He did not come to be served, to put us to work. That is not the goal of the Gospel. He came to serve, to work for us, to buy us back out of death, to restore us to health that we might stand in His presence as His beloved, immaculate bride. That is the goal of the Gospel: that we would be His and live with Him in bliss forever. The goal of the Gospel is the Gospel itself. And thus cleansed and believing, the healed leper is praised by God. By faith the leper has become the son of God in whom He is well-pleased.

Conclusion

God's Word for our lives is both Law and Gospel. Even though we have not kept the Law in its fullness, God has loved us perfectly. He speaks and it is so. He has kept His promise: He is our God. He has forgiven our sins in Jesus Christ. His love surpasses His wrath, "visiting the iniquity of the fathers on the children to the third and the fourth generation of those who hate" Him, "but showing steadfast love to thousands of those who love" Him and keep His commandments (Exodus 20:5–6). He gave us Ten Commandments, but His love is to a thousand generations, that is ten to the third power, or ten to the power of God.

Closing Prayer

Gracious God, I thank You for the opportunity to attend classes for a more thorough study of Your Word. Such instruction is the gift of Your pure mercy. Enable me to appreciate this privilege fully and to apply myself faithfully to the study of these lessons. Enlighten my understanding by Your Holy Spirit. Teach me the profound meaning of my Baptism, and lead me to a stronger faith.

I thank You for the faithful pastors and teachers who lead me and my classmates in Your way. We are gathered as members of Your family by the action of Your Spirit. Oh, keep us close to you and to one another by the power of Your holy Gospel! Help us to hear and learn Your Word gladly, so that we may know the joy of a Christian life.

If at times we become frustrated in the course of our studies, strengthen and encourage us through Your Holy Spirit. Bless us always for the sake of Jesus, our Savior. Amen.

(*Lutheran Book of Prayer*, p.154)

Five and Ten: Keys to God's Word

Five

List the first five books of the Bible. Who wrote them? What is the significance of the number five?

Read the following passages: **Matthew 5:17; 7:12; 11:13; Luke 24:44; John 1:45; Acts 28:23;** and **Romans 3:21**. What is meant by the "Law and the Prophets"? What is the Law? Who are the Prophets? How is this connected to the five books of Moses? What numbers are added to get five?

Read **Genesis 3:15**. This passage is in the Law section of Scripture. Is it Law or Gospel? Who is it about? Who is Eve's first son? How is five implied? Read also **Colossians 1:13–20**.

Read God's instructions to Moses about the altar in **Exodus 27:1–2**. Why five cubits by five cubits? And why three high? What is the shape of the altar in your church? Does it have any decorations on the top of it? How many wounds did Jesus have?

Read **John 20:24–29**. How does Jesus convince Thomas that it is really Him? If you were trying to convince someone of your identity, how would you do it? How does that relate to Christian altars with five crosses carved on them? How does the number of Jesus' wounds relate to the books of Moses?

Read **Revelation 5:6**. What does "as though it had been slain" mean? Do you think anyone else in heaven looks "as though he had been slain"?

Read the following passages: **Psalms 41:13; 72:18–19; 89:52; 106:48;** and **150:1–6**. What do the passages have in common? Why would we bless the Lord? What is different about the fifth passage?

What does the word *bless mean*? Why do we say in the liturgy "Let us bless the Lord"? How can we bless the Lord? What does the word *alleluia* mean?

Read **Leviticus 14:1–32**. Why were lepers treated this way? Why was the ceremony to be declared "clean" so complicated and drawn-out? Do you remember the distinction about the types of laws in the Old Testament?

Look again at **Leviticus 14:14, 25**. What are the differences? What is the significance of marking the leper in these ways? Why put oil on top of the blood? What does the word *anoint* mean? When was Jesus anointed? When were you anointed?

Ten

Read **Luke 17:11–19**. How many lepers are involved in this account? How does this relate to **Leviticus 14**? Why does the Samaritan return? How does this relate to the Law?

Read the Ten commndments in **Exodus 34:27–29**. How many commandments are there

Read **Exodus 20:1–17**. Number the commandments from the Bible. How many are there? Compare that numbering to the numbering in the Small Catechism. Are there any repetitions in the Commandments?

5

Seven and Twelve: Numbers in Revelation

Lesson Focus

This lesson will look at the use of seven and twelve in the Book of Revelation. The numbers are similar in that they are both combinations of the number of God (three) and the number of creation (four). The combination of these numbers by addition or multiplication demonstrates fullness. They are used many times in the Bible, but Revelation especially uses them to describe God's people.

Opening Prayer

Almighty and everlasting God, You knit together Your faithful people of all times and places into one holy communion, the mystical body of Your Son, Jesus Christ. Grant us so to follow Your blessed saints in all virtuous and godly living that, together with them, we may come to the unspeakable joys You have prepared for those who love You; through Jesus Christ, our Lord, who lives and reigns with You and the Holy Spirit, one God, now and forever. Amen. (Collect for All Saints Day, *LSB Altar Book*, p. 984)

Seven

Read Revelation 1:1–20. How many times do you see the number seven? What are the groups of seven? What is the significance of the number seven? To whom does John write?

The number seven occurs twelve times in Revelation 1 (verses 4, 11, 12, 16, and 20). There are five things in groups of seven: the churches (4, 11, 20), the spirits (4), the angels (20), the lampstands (12, 20), and the stars (16, 20). In verse 20, it is explained that the lampstands are symbols of the churches and the stars are symbols of their angels. We will argue that the seven spirits are the Holy Spirit. It is unclear if these five groups of seven are meant to convey something of the Word of God by referring us back to the books of Moses.

The vision contains two groups of seven: the churches and the angels. At the end of the section, they are placed side by side and seem to be doubled. "The seven stars are the angels of the seven churches, and the seven lampstands are the seven churches" (Revelation 1:20b). This doubling and repetition implies an idea of fullness or abundance. At the end of Job, Job gets back double of all he lost (Job 42:10). By doubling the churches and their angels, we get the number four, which is a number of creation like two. God created the churches and their angels. He continues to provide for them.

In Lesson 1, we learned that the number seven is a compound number, consisting of the number of God (three) plus the number of creation (four). It is a prime number and therefore indicates fullness or completion. It is also reminiscent of the creation in the number of days of the week.

The Book of Revelation consists of three parts: an introduction (1:1–3:22), the prophetic "message proper (4:1–22:5), and an epilogue (22:6–21)" (*Concordia Commentary: Revelation*, p. 9). The introduction is made up of chapter 1 and then letters dictated by God for John to write to the angels of each church (chapters 2–3). There is no compelling reason not to think that John sent the entire book to the seven churches (Ephesus, Smyrna, Pergamum, Thyatira, Sardis, Philadelphia, and Laodicea) rather than simply the sub-letter addressed to each church in chapters 2–3.

In any case, the places John names are real. While the churches are symbolic and stand in the stead of all churches, or all Christians, they are also historic. Each of those places had a Christian congregation in the first century when John saw his vision. The number seven is literal. There are literally seven churches. But the number seven is also symbolic. These weren't the only churches in Asia. It seems the number was chosen deliberately. The seven churches might represent the complete church on earth. The problems, sins, and weaknesses those churches suffered are common not only to all Christian congregations but also to individual congregations (1 Corinthians 10:13). Even though John is directed to write to the angel (singular) of each church, in the course of the dictation the plural is often used, such as in the first letter (Revelation 2:7), "He who has an ear, let him hear what the Spirit says to the churches." Thus it makes the most sense to understand that John sent the entire thing not only to all seven churches listed but also to all of Christendom—and we do well to apply these things to ourselves. We should recognize that John is writing to us and that he is also writing about us.

Read Revelation 1:4–7. What is the purpose of this part of the letter? Can you see God's personal name YHWH in verse 4? How is the Trinity expressed? How many spirits are before God's throne? Who are they?

In verse 4, John greets the churches and says "Grace to you and peace from Him who is and who was and who is to come." This description of God contains the verb *to be*, the verb that is God's Name. The participle used for *who is* is the same word that the Greek Old Testament uses to translate YHWH (see Lesson 2). In any case, John casts the verb *to be* in three tenses: present, past, and future. Some early Christian commentators saw this as trinitarian. They understood "Him who is" to refer to the Father, "who was" to refer to the Word that became flesh, the Son, and "who is to come" to refer to the Comforter, the Holy Spirit (see *Concordia Commentary: Revelation*, p.39). If those commentators are right, then the personal name of God has been cast by John into a distinct and deliberate trinitarian formulation. That is certainly an appealing idea and finds much merit when compared to Exodus 3:14. The problem with this interpretation comes in discerning what John then means by the seven spirits before God's throne and why He repeats also greetings from the Son in Revelation 1:5.

That problem is solved if "Him who is and who was and who is to come" is seen as a reference to the Father. In his commentary on Revelation, Brighton sees a theological principal at work in Revelation—the Father is the first among equals. John begins with greetings from the Father for, even though Jesus Christ and His work are the focus of the book, the message ultimately comes from the Father. Brighton notices that the participle translated as "who is" in verse 4 is used five times in Revelation (1:4, 8; 4:8; 11:17; and 16:5). He argues that all five times it refers to the Father. The reference to the second person is then obvious in verse 5 and the third person also becomes clear in "the seven spirits who are before His throne."

These seven spirits seem best identified with the Holy Spirit since they are sandwiched between explicit statements and persons of God, "Him who is" in verse 4 and Jesus Christ in verse 5. If these were the seven angels symbolized by the stars a little later, they might be before God's throne, but why would John bring greetings from them when He is about to bring greetings to them? Some have suggested they are the seven archangels, as listed in Jewish tradition in the apocryphal book 1 Enoch 19:1; 20:1–7, but there is simply no evidence for this (see *Concordia Commentary: Revelation*, p.41). The best argument is that these seven spirits are a symbolic way of portraying the Holy Spirit (v. 10). In Isaiah 11:2, the Holy Spirit who will rest upon the Messiah has seven attributes: (1) of the Lord, (2) of wisdom, (3) of understanding, (4) of counsel, (5) of might, (6) of knowledge, and (7) of the fear of the LORD. In Zechariah 3:9–4:10, Zechariah sees a vision of a rock with seven eyes. These eyes are the "eyes of the Lord." They see "the whole earth." The number seven here seems to indicate more than completion or fullness. Like the seven eyes and the seven gifts, it also indicates perfection. Thus the perfect spirit is the Holy Spirit (see *Concordia Commentary: Revelation*, pp. 41–42).

By either interpretation, John begins the letter with a trinitarian blessing that is tied to the number seven.

In Revelation 1:20, we read that "the seven stars are the angels of the seven churches." Who or what are these angels? Look ahead to Revelation 2:1. To whom is the letter addressed?

The letters in chapters 2 and 3 are addressed to the angels of each church. Who or what these angels are is not clear and is debated. There are three distinct possibilities. The first is that the angels are actually the pastors. While in English we almost always use the word *angel* to mean a supernatural, spiritual being, in Greek the word *angel* is simply a word for messenger. Pastors are God's messengers. God tells them what to tell the congregations they serve. The second possibility is that these are heavenly beings like the beings who announced the birth of Jesus to shepherds (Luke 2:13) and may even be some sort of personal guardian angel (Matthew 18:10) given to each congregation. The final possibility is to see the angels as symbols of an overarching character or personality of each congregation.

Brighton takes the position that it is best to take the second understanding but allows for the possibility of the first as well. The last possibility has no real evidence in the book or in the rest of the Bible. Sometimes God has used heavenly beings to convey His message. The angel of Jesus Christ made the revelation known to John (Revelation 1:1). That angel was not human. God used heavenly, non-human angels to give the Law to Moses on Mount Sinai (Acts 7:38, 53; Galatians 3:19; Hebrews 2:2), to announce Jesus' birth (Matthew 1:20; Luke 2:1–27; 2:8–9), and to proclaim the resurrection (Matthew 28:2–7). So the idea that these seven angels fit into what we normally think of as angels fits with what we know about angels and the context of Revelation.

Nonetheless, we also know that the prophets often spoke for the Lord. The phrase "thus says the Lord" is used 414 times in the Old Testament! God sends us pastors today for the same purpose. St. Paul writes, "For what we proclaim is not ourselves, but Jesus Christ as Lord, with ourselves as your servants for Jesus' sake" (2 Corinthians 4:5). We are used to hearing the pastor say: "I, as a called and ordained servant of the Word, announce the grace of God to all of you, and in the stead and by the command of my Lord Jesus Christ I forgive you all your sins in the name of the Father and of the Son and of the Holy Spirit" (*LW*, p.137). (See also the order of Individual Confession and Absolution in *Lutheran Worship* on pages 310–311.) If the angels were the pastors of these seven congregations, then it would have been very easy for John to send the book to them and have them read it to their congregations, much more so than if they were heavenly beings.

Whatever these angels are, whether they are human agents in the form of pastors or heavenly beings, the letters are meant for the people in the churches. God sends His Word to them. Again, the fact that there are seven of them means not only that each church is cared for but also that all the churches, the full number of churches, are cared for.

Divide the seven letters in Revelation 2–3 among the group. Have each group or individual read its letter and fill out the outline summary, then compare their findings.

The letters are (1) 2:1–7; (2) 2:8–11; (3) 2:12–17; (4) 2:18–29; (5) 3:1–6; (6) 3:7–13; and (7) 3:14–22.

You may assign the individual letters, have the charts filled out, and then re-read the letters as a group prior to or in response to the report of the summary or you may simply let the reports suffice to save time. The goal of this exercise is to see that the letters come from Christ and are immediately applicable to the reader. The letters serve as a sevenfold description of the person of Jesus Christ, a description of the Church on this side of glory, a call to repentance, and a promise of the life to come. The sevenfold character and repetition of these same things, with different words and images, is meant to convey fullness. The answers to the questions for the individual letters are below. Your students may summarize slightly differently due to differences in translation or interpretation.

After the summaries are presented to the group, the students should see that the letters are all very similar and all convey the same message—repent. Besides that, the letters also tell us quite a bit about who Jesus is and who we are in Him, but the most significant thing is always who Jesus is.

The sevenfold description of Jesus taken from the letters shows us a lot of comforting details. They give us a multifaceted description of our Savior. In the first letter, Jesus is described as holding the seven stars and walking among the seven lampstands (2:1). He is among the churches, with His people. In the second letter, He is called the first and the last and the one who died and came back to life (2:8). He is the Savior who has sacrificed Himself for us. In the third letter, we are told He has the sharp two-edged sword (2:12). He has the Word of God. He divides death from life. In the fourth letter, He is presented as the Son of God with eyes like a flame of fire and feet like burnished bronze (2:18). The title "Son of God" hearkens back to His Baptism, where the crowd heard the Father claim Jesus as His Son. Jesus' Baptism was His anointing (or messiah-ing—see lesson 4) (Matthew 3:13–17). In the fifth letter, He has the seven spirits of God and holds the seven stars. The seven spirits of God are the Holy Spirit (Revelation 1:4) and the seven stars are the angels of the churches. The sixth letter describes Jesus as the Holy One, the True One, the One who has the key of David, who opens and no one will shut, who shuts and no one will open (3:7). The seventh finishes with Jesus as the amen, the faithful and true witness, the beginning of God's creation (3:14). The word *amen* is the Hebrew word for *truth*. The Hebrew and Greek believers of the New Testament used this word in the same way we use it—as a closing to a prayer. The idea is that we are attesting to the truth of the prayer. Calling Jesus the amen not only means that He is the truth (John 14:6) but also that He is the last word and the response to Christian prayer. Every Christian prayer that closes with amen is prayer in Jesus' name, for He is the truth. Each of the descriptions of Jesus from these seven letters is sufficient of itself, but when the entire sevenfold description is taken as a piece, it presents a very full witness to the work and character of our Savior.

The same thing can be done with the calls to repentance and the promises that Jesus makes to those who heed the warning to repent and conquer. After the description of the person and work of Jesus, the most significant idea in these letters is the character of the Church on earth. The letters that are sent to the seven churches are about those churches. The number seven should help us to see that these are not merely descriptions of the institutions or congregations at that time. Both the number seven and the great similarity between the different churches described demonstrate that these descriptions, calls to repentance, and promises are to all Christians, to the full and true Church, that is, not the congregations or buildings, but to the total number of true believers. As descriptions of the true Church, these are also descriptions of the individual Christian. On this side of glory, we are both saint and sinner, and what the letters reveal about the seven churches in Asia are also revelations and warnings for us.

The letters reveal that the Church endures in patience, yet at times abandons her first love (first letter). She is suffering for the truth and yet still afraid of suffering (second letter). She holds fast to Christ's name and clings to the faith, yet she will also tolerate false teachers (third letter). She has love, faith, and service, but will also engage in immorality (fourth letter.) She is pure, but her works are not yet complete (fifth letter). She keeps God's word, but has little power (sixth letter), and at times can be lukewarm and indecisive about whether she belongs to Christ or not (seventh letter). Again, this sevenfold description shows a full picture of the Church, comforted yet conflicted, encouraged and praised but also warned. Thus the last two questions for every letter— "Could this letter be sent to your congregation?" and "Could it be sent to you personally?"—is yes. These descriptions describe us as sinner and saint. The call to repentance and warning are for us—and the promise of the reward to come is also for us.

Answers for the outline:

1. To whom is the letter addressed? The angel of Ephesus
   How is the sender described? The One who holds the seven stars and walks among the seven lampstands
   Who is the sender? Christ
   What does He see that is good? Patient endurance
   What does He see that is bad? They abandoned the love they had at first
   Is there a call to repent? Yes
   What is the closing promise? The one who conquers will eat of the tree of life.
2. To whom is the letter addressed? The angel of Smyrna
   How is the sender described? The first and the last, He who died and came to life
   Who is the sender? Christ
   What does He see that is good? Suffering
   What does He see that is bad? Fear
   Is there a call to repent? Yes, but subtle: "Do not be afraid."
   What is the closing promise? The one who conquers will not be hurt by the second death.
3. To whom is the letter addressed? The angel of Pergamum
   How is the sender described? He who has the sharp two-edged sword
   Who is the sender? Christ
   What does He see that is good? They hold fast to Christ's name and have not denied the faith.
   What does He see that is bad? They have some false teachers.
   Is there a call to repent? Yes
   What is the closing promise? The one who conquers (Christ) will be given some of the hidden manna and a white stone with a new name.
4. To whom is the letter addressed? The angel of Thyratira
   How is the sender described? The Son of God who has eyes like a flame of fire and whose feet are like burnished bronze
   Who is the sender? Christ
   What does He see that is good? Love, faith, service, and patient endurance
   What does He see that is bad? They tolerate a false teacher who teaches sexual immorality.
   Is there a call to repent? Yes
   What is the closing promise? The one who conquers (Christ) will be given authority over the nations and will give them the morning star.
5. To whom is the letter addressed? The angel of Sardis
   How is the sender described? He who has the seven spirits of God and seven stars.
   Who is the sender? Christ
   What does He see that is good? Some have not soiled their garments
   What does He see that is bad? Have a reputation for being alive but are dead, works are not complete.
   Is there a call to repent? Yes.
   What is the closing promise? The one who conquers will be clothed in white garments. His name will be written in the Book of Life and Christ will confess it before the Father.
6. To whom is the letter addressed? The angel of Philadelphia
   How is the sender described? The Holy One, the True One, who has the key of David, who opens and no one will shut, who shuts and no one will open
   Who is the sender? Christ
   What does He see that is good? They have kept His word and not denied His name.
   What does He see that is bad? They have but little power.
   Is there a call to repent? Yes, but subtle: "Hold fast to what you have."

What is the closing promise? The one who conquers will be made a pillar of the temple and will never leave it. God's name will be written on him.

7. To whom is the letter addressed? The angel of Laodicea

How is the sender described? The Amen, the faithful and true witness, the beginning of God's creation

Who is the sender? Christ

What does He see that is good? Nothing!

What does He see that is bad? They are lukewarm, blind to their need.

Is there a call to repent? Yes

What is the closing promise? The one who conquers will sit with Christ on His throne.

There are more sevens in Revelation than this. The entire book is set up around seven. After this introduction, the main section of the prophecy unfolds as three sevenfold visions (6:1–8:5; 8:6–11:19; and 15:1–16:21). Encourage the students to read further on their own and to keep a lookout for seven.

Twelve

Read Revelation 21:9–27. What does this city represent? How many gates are there in the new Jerusalem? Why so many? How are they named? What of the foundation stones?

In verse 9, one of the seven angels tells John to come with him, and he will show him the "Bride, the wife of the Lamb." He shows him the "holy city Jerusalem coming down out of heaven." This city represents the Church. (See also Matthew 9:15 where Jesus describes Himself as the Bridegroom and the parable in Matthew 25.)

There are twelve gates in the new Jerusalem. They are named for the twelve tribes of Israel. The Church is again tied to the tribes of Israel even as it was earlier when John saw 12,000 from each tribe to equal 144,000 (see Lesson 1). Normally, a walled city in the ancient world only had one gate since gates were weak points in the defense. The point of a wall was to keep invaders out. The wall around the new Jerusalem is different. It remains a stronghold of protection but the city comes down from heaven after the defeat of Satan (Revelation 20:7–10). There is no longer any threat. With Satan bound there is no one to hurt us, nothing left in creation to attack us. The wall is not needed for defense, but our God is still strong. There are many gates because the city is open. There is nothing to fear.

The number of gates is not accidental, nor is their placement. John sees that the city is square (21:16). It has four equal sides, each 12,000 stadia (about 1400 miles) long. The walls are also 12,000 stadia high. They are as high as they are wide so that the walls themselves, like the city, are square: 12,000 by 12,000. The city is equal on every side horizontally and vertically. The walls are 144 cubits thick, which is also twelve squared. To further reinforce its connection to creation, each wall faces one of the cardinal directions and, to connect to the divine, each wall has three gates. While it isn't stated explicitly in the text, these must have been evenly spaced in the walls. Thus each wall could be further divided into four equal sections between the three gates. Some scholars have suggested that the whole layout of the city is meant to bring to mind what we learned of the number three in Lesson 2 and the number four in Lesson 3. Twelve is the number of the earth and creation (four) times the number of God (three). By having three gates in each wall, the city has a divine presence on each side. The gates, however, are not weak points as in a traditional earthly city. They are strong points as St. Paul writes: "When I am weak, then I am strong" (2 Corinthians 12:10). So also the defeat and death of Jesus Christ on the cross became not only His victory but the victory for all creation (John 12:32).

The twelve gates are named for the twelve tribes even as the twelve foundation stones are named for the twelve apostles. Like the twenty-four elders from Revelation 4 that we learned about in Lesson 1, these gates remind us of the unity of the Old and New Testaments. God's people are one. His promise to all of them is the same. The believers who lived prior to the resurrection of Jesus Christ were saved by a forward-looking faith that waited for the promised Messiah. We are saved by faith that looks back and sees the fulfillment of that same promise in Jesus the Messiah. Moreover, these gates match Ezekiel's vision of the new Jerusalem (Ezekiel 48:30–34). He also saw the new Jerusalem with twelve gates named for the tribes, with its four walls oriented to the four cardinal directions. John's vision is not substantially different, but adds more details. John's vision echoes what Paul explained in Ephesians 2:19–22—that the Church is "built on the foundation of the apostles and prophets, Christ Jesus Himself being the cornerstone" (Ephesians 2:20). With gates and foundation stones, we have the twenty-four, twelve doubled or eight times three. In either case, we have a number that indicates abundance, perfection, and completion. Twelve patriarchs and twelve apostles is more than twice as good. It is perfect.

Conclusion

The numbers seven and twelve are numbers of completion and perfection. They are God's numbers, but He uses them to count His Church. He gives and applies His numbers to His people. He adds Himself to them (3+4=7) and He multiplies them by Himself (3X4=12). Both numbers indicate that God joins Himself to believers in grace.

Closing Prayer

Lord God, our King on heaven's throne,
Our Father, the Almighty One.
O Lord, the Sole-begotten One,
Lord Jesus Christ, the Father's Son,
True God from all eternity,
O Lamb of God to You we flee.

This truth divine, this mystery
The angels sing adoringly.
By all creation, far and wide;
You, Lord, are ever glorified;
For all Your people sing Your praise
Now and through everlasting days.

("All Glory Be to God Alone," *LW* 210:3, 6; *LSB* 948:3)

Seven and Twelve: Numbers in Revelation

Seven

Read **Revelation 1:1–20**. How many times do you see the number seven? What are the groups of seven? What is the significance of the number seven? To whom does John write?

Read **Revelation 1:4–7**. What is the purpose of this part of the letter? Can you see God's personal name YHWH in **verse 4**? How is the Trinity expressed? How many spirits are before God's throne? Who are they?

In **Revelation 1:20**, we read that "the seven stars are the angels of the seven churches." Who or what are these angels? Look ahead to **Revelation 2:1**. To whom is the letter addressed?

Divide the seven letters in **Revelation 2–3** among the group. Have each group or individual read its letter and fill out the outline summary, then compare their findings.

The letters are (1) **2:1–7**
(2) **2:8–11**
(3) **2:12–17**
(4) **2:18–29**
(5) **3:1–6**
(6) **3:7–13**
(7) **3:14–22**

Twelve

Read **Revelation 21:9–27**. What does this city represent? How many gates are there in the new Jerusalem? Why so many? How are they named? What of the foundation stones?

Letters to the Churched —Summary Outline

Bible passage:

To whom is the letter addressed?

How is the sender described?

Who is the sender?

What does He see that is good?

What does He see that is bad?

Is there a call to repent?

What is the closing promise?

Could this letter be sent to your congregation?

Could it be sent to you personally?

6 Forty and Eight: A Generation of Mercy and the New Creation

Lesson Focus

The number forty is often repeated in the Bible. God uses it to show the age of men and how they pass away. He also uses it to connect the promise of His love and deliverance in Jesus Christ to man's frailty. As frail as man is, God is strong and a new creation is coming.

Opening Prayer

Almighty and eternal God, according to Your strict judgment You condemned the unbelieving world through the flood, yet according to Your great mercy You preserved believing Noah and his family, eight souls in all. You drowned hard-hearted Pharaoh and all his host in the Red Sea, yet led Your people Israel through the water on dry ground, foreshadowing this washing of Your Holy Baptism. Through the Baptism in the Jordan of Your beloved Son, our Lord Jesus Christ, You sanctified and instituted all waters to be a blessed flood and a lavish washing away of sin. Through Jesus Christ, our Lord. Amen.

(*Lutheran Service Book Agenda,* p. 14)

The Generation Gap

What is a generation? How long is it? How old were your parents when you were born? Read Numbers 32:13.

A generation is a group of people who are the same age or from the same era. It is usually determined by the average length of years between parents and their children. Everyone in your class is in the same generation, even though you are not all exactly the same age. Likewise, all your parents are in the same generation. But as we will see, that number and the definition gets fuzzy quickly—except in the Bible, where it is defined for us.

In Numbers 32:13, we read that the Israelites had to wander in the desert for forty years until the entire generation was gone. That passage helps establish the length of a generation. It is forty years. To put it into our definition above, that means mothers and fathers are separated from their children by forty years. It rarely works out this way. Most people these days have children in their twenties or thirties. It rarely worked out in the Bible either, since people had babies then as early as fifteen or sixteen and some people (Abraham and Sarah) had babies when they were very old. The idea in Numbers 32 of making a generation forty years is a little different. It is based on how long it would take until the youngest adult living would be dead. The point of the punishment was to purge Israel. If the age of the youngest adult was twenty and life expectancy was sixty, then all the adults living at the time of the curse would have been dead by the end of forty years. It is like this: if we want to leave our hometown today and come back when no one who is now an adult will still be here, we wait forty years. God explains the forty years of wandering earlier when He says, "Surely none of the men who came up out of Egypt, from twenty years old and upward, shall see the land that I swore to give to Abraham, to Isaac, and to Jacob, because they have not wholly followed Me" (Numbers 32:11).

Despite this, it is a bit hard for us to think of forty as the length of a generation. It is not that large a gap in most of our families. Most of us were born to our parents when they were in their twenties or young thirties. If you look at the spread it works better. Instead of considering only your own parents, take the ages of the parents of all the students at your high school. The youngest mom of the youngest freshman can be as young as thirty-one. The oldest father of the oldest senior can easily be sixty-six. In that context, forty seems more reasonable. The requirement in the exodus for forty years was so long because God wanted all the adults removed. Forty years made sure it happened.

Another way of looking at it is to consider how close a person of one age is to people of other ages. The younger you are, the more significant small differences in age. Twenty years apart sounds like a big difference, but we still might say they are in the same generation. We would never say that of a sixty-year-old and a twenty-year-old. Forty years apart, even though it might be the difference between grandparent and grandchild and not parent and child, is far enough apart to surely be two distinct generations. So again, the idea with forty years in the desert is a complete and total cleansing.

The distance between fathers and sons, mothers and daughters, usually varies between twenty and forty. But the Bible has assigned forty as the length of a generation. The number forty is a compound number. It is the number of man or creation (four) times ten. Ten conveys the idea of perfection and completion. Forty years is a solid number. The Israelites wandered in the desert for an actual forty years. That is a literal number. It is also a symbolic number. It was roughly the amount of time it would take for a generation of adults to die off. It showed the cost of their rebellion—a full generation was excluded from the Promised Land. As serious as it was, forty is not all there is. It is only half a man's lifespan. It is a huge loss, but not all they have. At the end of forty years, God's people came into the Promised Land. They were in the desert for forty years. They will be in the Promised Land forever.

Noah's Saving Ark

While Noah and his family were in the dark, God sent rain for forty days and forty nights. Can you think of any other times that the Bible speaks of "forty days and forty nights"? Read Matthew 4:1–2; 1 Kings 19:7–8; and Deuteronomy 9:9. Why fast for forty days and nights?

Jesus, Elijah, and Moses all fasted for forty days and forty nights. We might also recall that there were forty days between our Lord's resurrection and His ascension (Acts 1:3). The prophet Elijah also fasted for forty days and forty nights. When Jesus fasted, He was hungry. When Elijah fasted, he was not hungry. After destroying the false prophets of Baal (1 Kings 18:22–46), he got scared and ran from the wicked queen Jezebel. He hid in the desert and asked to die. The Lord did not grant his request. God had once sent Elijah food by way of ravens (1 Kings 17:1–6); now God sent him food by way of an angel. Elijah went in the strength of that food, that is, without any further food or drink, for forty days and forty nights (1 Kings 19:8). Moses also endured three fasts of forty days and forty nights at the giving of the Law at Sinai (Exodus 24:18 and 34:28). The chronology is clearest in his description in Deuteronomy 9 and 10 where Moses prepared the people to cross into the Promised Land. He was on the mountain the first time getting the Law for forty days and forty nights (Exodus 24:18 and Deuteronomy 9:9). While there, he fasted. When Moses came down from the mountain, he found the golden calf and broke the tablets God had given him. He then lay prostrate on the ground for forty days and forty nights (Deuteronomy 9:18 and 25) as public penance for the sins of the people. Finally, Moses went back up on the mountain to get new tablets and was there again for forty days and forty nights (Exodus 34:28 and Deuteronomy 10:10).

All of these forty day and forty night fasts are meant to recall Israel's wandering in the desert. They are all meant as a kind of purging and preparing for a new era. Jesus is anointed by John the Baptist and about to begin His public ministry when He fasts. Elijah has just defeated the prophets of Baal. Moses will come down from the mountain with the Law. All of these events also take place after the flood and call to mind the rainy destruction of the earth. Finally, all of these events have an end. They do not bring about destruction. Life comes through in the end.

Liturgically, we echo these forties around Easter. We always observe Easter on Sunday, the day of the week that Jesus rose. When we count backwards forty days from Easter, we always land on a Wednesday. Starting at Ash Wednesday, we observe forty days of Lent. It reminds us of Jesus' time of fasting in the desert as well as echoing the forty-day events that came before. When we count forward from Easter forty days, we always land on a Thursday. That is the day we remember Jesus' ascension to the Father after He appeared to His disciples and opened the Scriptures to them. Forty is the full number of man's days, so it is always a good number for preparation.

Review the story of the flood by reading Genesis 6–8. Think about the numbers. How big was the ark? How long was the flood from start to finish? How long were they on the ark? How many people were on the ark? How many animals?

Noah entered the ark one week before the flood began (Genesis 7:10). The flood began on the seventeenth day of the second month (Genesis 7:11) and Noah left the ark on the twenty-seventh day of the second month (Genesis 8:14) the following year. Assuming a 365-day year, the flood then lasted 375 days. Noah and his family were on the ark one week prior, so they were on the ark 382 days. There were eight people on the ark, Noah and his wife and their three sons with their three wives (Genesis 8:15–16). They are not actually counted in Genesis. Peter does that, "in the days of Noah, while the ark was being prepared, in which a few, that is, eight persons, were brought safely through water" (1 Peter 3:20b). There were seven of each clean animal and two of each unclean, one male and one female. More clean animals were brought because they were used for food and for sacrifices and at least one pair of each species had to remain at the end to repopulate the earth (Genesis 8:20).

The ark was three-hundred cubits long, fifty cubits wide, and thirty cubits high (Genesis 6:15). The cubit's length was not standard in the ancient world. It varied from place to place and time to time, but even when it was standardized, such as the distance from the elbow to the tip of the longest finger, the length would vary from person to person. That is not to say it could be any length at all. A cubit was never less than eighteen or more than twenty-four inches. If we take the longest possible unit the ark was six-hundred feet long, one-hundred feet wide, and sixty feet high. That is about the height of a six story house, two football fields long, and as wide as four houses side by side. As described in Genesis, the ark was simply a rectangle, but it may have had some shape to it and even been shaped something like a boat.

Assuming these dimensions of the ark, it would have had a capacity of 3.6 million cubic feet. An ordinary cattle car on the railroad carries eighteen to twenty head of cattle, or sixty to eighty hogs, or eighty to one hundred sheep. At 3.6 million cubic feet, the ark was big enough for ten thousand of those cars. That means it could have carried as much as two hundred thousand cows or 1 million sheep. It should be noted, though, that most animals aren't as large as sheep. Think of squirrels and rabbits and field mice. Certainly there are a few large animals, such as elephants and giraffes, but there are not many. Noah only had to bring two of each of those. Another possibility is that Noah brought babies of the larger animals instead of adults. Since we know that individual types of animals descend from common species, it is reasonable to assume that Noah only took one pair of each particular species. For instance, perhaps Noah brought only one pair of dogs—not a pair each of Dalmatians, Labrador retrievers, poodles, and so forth. Likewise there was probably only one pair of cows on the ark, not separate pairs of Herefords, Brown Swiss, Holsteins, and Angus.

There was a lot of room on the ark. It may be that there was plenty of room for all the animals, the people, and for food. Even so, the entire event was miraculous. That is really the answer to how all the animals fit on the ark, how they got along with each other for 375 days, and the like. It was a real, physical hardship for Noah and his family. God used Noah to provide for the animals. None of it, from the building, to the loading, to the daily care and waiting, to the off-loading could have been done without God's constant presence and protection. So also after the flood, God blessed these animals and Noah so that they multiplied and again filled the earth.

It is worth noting at this point that all humans are descended from Noah, his three sons, and their wives. To speak of different races of men is somewhat misleading. The differences between those of Latino, Asian, African, or European descent are only cosmetic. We are not different races. We are all humans, all descended from the same stock. So there can be no moral argument or complaint against so-called "interracial marriage" any more than there can be arguments against people with different-colored eyes marrying. It may be true that marriages of mixed ethnicity will have many barriers to overcome both in terms of understanding one another's cultures and in terms of finding acceptance in an imperfect and often prejudiced society. But history has taught us that society has been enriched by such brave souls and that these marriages have done a great deal of good in encouraging tolerance and true compassion. Remember that the ancient kings always forged alliances with marriage. Such "mixed" marriages promoted peace. The exchange and blending of earthly cultures always benefits those involved. Racism has no place in Christianity.

In the context of the flood, the number forty becomes a number of judgment. It is very similar to Israel's forty-year sojourn in the wilderness. At the time of the flood, humanity was evil. It had to be destroyed. God sent forty days and forty nights of rain. He could have done it in an hour, but he poured down this wrath for the full time of man, four times ten. What He created in six days, He took away in forty. Man's days are limited. He is weak. He cannot endure such wrath. But the forty days and forty nights of rain are not without context. Even as the wilderness wandering came to an end, so too did the rain. And even as God fed the people with manna and quail during the wandering, so too in the midst of God's anger with humanity is His compassion and concern for His servant Noah and his family. Before He destroyed the world, He provided for them. God's sadness at having made men was for their violence (Genesis 6:6–7, 11). Is He sad when the demons pick on one another? No. Let them fight. It does not concern Him. God is sad for the violence of men because He cares for Noah. The destruction comes for Noah's good. God spares Noah and his family from these evil people and their temptations. He gives Noah a chance to start over.

Why does God spare Noah? Verse 9 says that Noah was righteous and blameless in his generation, that He walked with God. Does that mean that Noah earned God's favor, that his good works proved his love to God and convinced God to save him? No! Genesis 6:8 is the pivotal verse. The ESV translates "Noah found favor in the eyes of the LORD" (Genesis 6:8). It would be better translated here either as "Noah found grace with God" or "Noah found mercy with God." The Greek Old Testament translates the Hebrew word *CHEN* as *XAPIS*. It does not mean "God's pleasure." It does mean God found something pleasing in Noah. In verse 12, Moses records that God saw that all flesh was corrupt. All flesh includes Noah! Why then was Noah spared? He was spared because of God's mercy or grace. God chose Noah not because of who Noah was but because of who God is. He is the God who is gracious. In verse 18, God makes a promise. He will establish a covenant with Noah, that is, He will make a promise. The promise is that Noah and his sons, his wife, and his son's wives will come into the ark. They will be safe. They do not come into the ark as their part of the bargain! That is what God does for them. He says, "I will establish my covenant with you, and you shall come into the ark, you, your sons, your wife, and your sons' wives with you" (Genesis 6:18). God spares Noah in His mercy, for the sake of the innocent suffering and death of the Messiah to come. It is the same reason Adam and Eve were spared, the same reason Moses would lead the people out of Egypt, the same reason that we worship God in Spirit and truth. Jesus died and Jesus lives and we are spared.

A New Sign for a New Covenant

Read 1 Peter 3:18–22. What is the significance of the number eight?

Peter expounds the meaning of both the

flood and the saving of Noah for us. The spirits in prison are the spirits of men in Hell. They are there because they rejected the name of the Only-Begotten One. "Whoever believes in Him is not condemned, but whoever does not believe is condemned already, because he has not believed in the name of the only Son of God" (John 3:18). They were disobedient in the days of Noah and would not heed Noah's warning or invitation. They did not recognize God in His Word or would not accept Him. So they were destroyed. But Noah was spared. Noah and seven others, in both body and soul, were carried safely over the carnage and brought to a new earth. Baptism corresponds to the flood—for Baptism is water that saves us. It destroys the old man. "We were buried therefore with [Christ] by baptism into death" (Romans 6:4a). That same water carries the new man to safety, above the destruction, and joins us to Christ's resurrection. Peter writes that Baptism is not a physical washing, a removal of dirt from the body. Rather, it appeals "to God for a good conscience, through the resurrection of Jesus Christ" (1 Peter 3:21).

Read Genesis 17:11–12. What day did circumcision take place? Read Colossians 2:11–14. What is the "circumcision made without hands"? Is there any significance to the number of the people on the ark to tie the ark to circumcision and therefore Baptism?

Moses told us who was on the ark. Peter counted them. There were eight. Eight was also the number for circumcision. All Jewish males were circumcised eight days after birth (Genesis 17:12). Paul connects Baptism to circumcision in his letter to the Colossians. The circumcision of Christ is the new circumcision. It is "made without hands." We might call Baptism circumcision's replacement. It is the new sign of the covenant, the promise of God. Baptism is not a violent, bloody cutting off of flesh, but rather a cleansing by water. It joins the believer to the death and resurrection of Christ. The believer is buried and raised with Him (Colossians 2:12; Romans 6:4). We were dead in our sins. We were uncircumcised, unclean, yet through Baptism God made us alive together with Christ, "Having forgiven us all our trespasses, by canceling the record of debt that stood against us with its legal demands. This He set aside, nailing it to the cross" (Colossians 2:13–14). This new sign is not merely for males. It is for everyone in all nations (Matthew 28:19). Both Peter and Paul tie Baptism's power to the resurrection (1 Peter 3:21; Romans 6:4; and Colossians 2:12). Paul names Baptism as the sign of the circumcision without hands, that is, without violence, in Colossians 2. Peter invokes circumcision by the use of the number eight.

The eighth day is the day outside of the days of creation. It is the new day, the day that breaks the pattern. God created the universe in six days. He rested on the seventh. The Old Testament ceremonial law required a constant counting of days. The seventh day, Saturday, was a day of rest and of hearing God's Word. That was a gift to the people, but it also required sacrifices and hardship. Forgetting to rest was a serious offense. It brought God's judgment down upon the offender. The tireless cycle of counting days was repeated over and over again. It was no accident that Our Lord completed His work for the new creation on the sixth day. He pronounced it was finished on the sixth day, on Friday, while He hung on the cross. That finished the new creation. He declared everything good once again. The Father's wrath was appeased. Order was restored. Then He gave up His soul. That is what it means to die a physical death. Physical death is the separation of the soul from the body. Jesus died the way all believers die. His soul ascended to heaven while His body was laid into the ground to await the resurrection. This is how He fulfilled the Law for us. He finished on the sixth day in a perfect reflection of the original creation, and then continued that image by resting in the grave for the final Sabbath, on the seventh day. Then He broke the pattern. He fulfilled the Law. He began new creation with a new day. He did not rise on the first day, as though the pattern was continuing. Instead, He rose and started the new day, the eighth day. Now every day is the day of the resurrection. The Law is fulfilled. It has nothing more to ask of us, to demand, and is emptied also of all accusations. Paul writes,

> One person esteems one day as better than another, while another esteems all days alike. Each one should be fully convinced in his own mind. The one who observes the day, observes it in honor of the Lord. The one who eats, eats in honor of the Lord, since he gives thanks to God, while the one who abstains, abstains in honor of the Lord and gives thanks to God. (Romans 14:5–6)

Because Jesus died and rose, all days are equal, all days are the eighth day, the day of God's covenant promise (circumcision) and the fulfillment of that promise (the resurrection).

When God commanded that circumcision take place on the eighth day, He was showing that the covenant put His people outside of time. Circumcision was outside the pattern. It placed the circumcised into the new creation. Peter saw this same significance in the number of souls on the ark. The number eight therefore draws its symbolism from the days of creation. But mathematics also comes into play. Eight is a number one better than the number of creation. It is creation (seven) or the full number of God and man (three plus four) plus one. This mathematical reality reinforces the idea of eight being outside of time and of creation.

In many churches, we see this connection between Baptism and eight in the design of their baptismal font. In traditional church architecture, it is common for baptismal fonts to have eight sides. The idea is that the shape would help us remember Baptism's connection to circumcision since Baptism is the sign of the new covenant, which joins us to the resurrection of Jesus Christ. The eight sides also remind us of the eight survivors of the flood who were saved through the waters. Less common is an attempt to make the pulpit into a pseudo-octagon. The pulpit is made to appear eight-sided even though it is always missing at least part of one side so that the preacher can actually enter into it. A few churches have taken this symbolism as far as architecture will allow. They have made their entire buildings into octagons!

Forty Years to Prepare for the New Age

Read what Paul did long after his conversion and missionary journeys had begun in Acts 21:26. Now read Acts 8:26–38. How long were the temple sacrifices valid after Jesus rose from the dead? What does the Ethiopian eunuch teach us about the Word given to those who were waiting for the Messiah outside Palestine?

We don't know the exact time of Our Lord's birth. The Bible tells us it was during the reign of Caesar Augustus (Luke 2:1). We do not know the exact time of our Lord's death and resurrection either. We know it was after the death of Herod the Great and during the time that Pontius Pilate was governor in Judah. That tells us that Jesus was about thirty years old when He laid down His life for us and the temple veil was torn in two. The Bible doesn't tell us that the veil was repaired, but temple services and sacrifices continued until the Romans destroyed the temple in 70 AD. So we know when temple services stopped. In other words, the temple stood and sacrifices were offered for approximately forty years after the resurrection.

Paul himself offered sacrifices in the temple during this time, as we read in Acts 21:26. Paul honored the temple, but he did not demand circumcision (Romans 3:30). He kept the Law in his freedom in Christ. He did not forbid circumcision. He forbids trust in it as an outward work (Romans 4:8–13). The time would come, however, when no more sacrifices could be offered. It needed to end. God's promise is no longer in the Passover lambs, in the ancient types. It is now in Christ (Hebrews 10:10). Circumcision might be kept in freedom, but how long could lambs be offered for the sins already removed by Jesus? Forty years. God allowed it for one generation. God, in His wisdom, allowed time for the Word of the Messiah to get out to wherever God's people were scattered.

The Ethiopian eunuch did not live in Palestine. He lived in Africa. We know he had at least part of the Old Testament since he was reading from the prophet Isaiah. Knowing what he did, the man from Ethiopia had come to Jerusalem, to the temple, to worship Isaiah's God. Jesus had already died and risen again. All things were complete. It was finished. Pentecost was over. But the eunuch did not know it. He had not yet heard the fulfillment of the Good News in Isaiah. He did not know the Messiah had been born in Bethlehem or the things He had suffered from the Sanhedrin. His hope and faith was the same as Isaiah's eight hundred years earlier. He was waiting for the Messiah whom God had promised would come like a sheep to the slaughter. God sent Phillip to tell him that this Messiah had come in the person of Jesus of Nazareth. Upon hearing the news, the eunuch was baptized.

There was a time in the Church's history when the church waited for the Messiah. They waited and believed.

> By faith Noah, being warned by God concerning events as yet unseen, in reverent fear constructed an ark for the saving of his household. By this He condemned the world and became an heir of the righteousness that comes by faith. (Hebrews 11:7)

Noah's faith and hope delivered to him what God would accomplish for him in time. His faith looked forward. Now that the Messiah has come and has been revealed to us, our faith looks back. The Church on both sides of the resurrection is saved in the same way: by the suffering, death, and resurrection of Jesus Christ. The Church on both sides of the resurrection receives this in the same way—by faith.

The eunuch in Acts 8 was still living in the hope of the Messiah to come. He had gone to Jerusalem and worshiped in accordance with the ceremonial law of the Old Testament. He did not know that this Law had already been completely fulfilled in and by Jesus Christ. So the Holy Spirit sent Phillip to tell him. Once he found out, he was baptized. He received the sign of the new covenant. But there were still others like the eunuch who were living according to faith. They believed that God was good and would send the Messiah for them. They were waiting. The temple remained valid for them. That is why Paul honored and participated in the temple sacrifices. God gave mankind forty years in His mercy. He gave the Christian Church one full generation to get the Good News out. Once that time was complete, He took away the temple. His presence is no longer there. We have no need of Jerusalem or the temple anymore. Jesus is present for us in His Word, in the waters of Holy Baptism, and in Holy Communion. This is where He has promised to be.

Read Matthew 24:1–14. What does Jesus say about the temple's future? How is what happened in AD 70 a testimony to the whole world? What is the temple that is torn down and rebuilt in three days?

God demonstrates that He is not contained in the buildings of men. As beautiful as Herod's temple was, and despite the fact that God was present there for His people, the temple was temporary. We do well to look at our own church buildings in the same way. God promises to be present for us in Word and Sacrament. He is there for us whether our churches are elaborate and beautiful or humble and simple. These buildings are special places. They are set aside as places to hear God's Word and to eat and drink the body and blood of Jesus. God communes with us in our churches. He forgives our sins in those places. That makes them special places. Still, they will burn on the Last Day. Not only is God not bound to these places, but these places are temporary. The beauty of heaven overshadows the beautiful things of this world. Heaven's reality is in no need of decoration or catechetical devices from men.

God removed His presence from the temple because the Law had been fulfilled. There is no more need for sacrifices. He is no longer present in the temple sacrifices. He is now present with Jews and Gentiles all over the world on the bloodless Christian altars of the resurrection. God destroyed the temple for this reason. He told us about it beforehand so that no one could doubt that these things have come to pass and that there is a new, indestructible temple.

> Jesus answered them, "Destroy this temple, and in three days I will raise it up." The Jews then said, "It has taken forty-six years to build this temple, and will you raise it up in three days?" But He was speaking about the temple of His body. (John 2:19–21)

Jesus says, "This gospel of the kingdom will be proclaimed throughout the whole world as a testimony to all nations" (Matthew 24:14). The Good News of the death and resurrection of Jesus Christ includes the destruction of Jerusalem. It is a warning, a call to repentance. This is what happens if the Word of God is rejected. The destruction also shows us the new and greater temple that He has built without hands and gives to us. The new temple is His body. He gives us the new temple to eat and drink in Holy Communion.

So also does Paul remind us: "Do you not know that you are God's temple and that God's Spirit dwells in you?" (1 Corinthians 3:16). You too were built without hands. You were baptized into Christ and were "born of water and the Spirit" (John 3:5). "That which is born of the flesh is flesh, and that which is born of the Spirit is spirit" (John 3:6). This Gospel of the new, rebuilt temple is preached where Jesus is preached. It is the Gospel.

There might be a temptation to see symbolism in the number seventy since that it is the year the temple was destroyed. But the reality is that God allowed one generation, forty years, to pass after the resurrection of Jesus before the temple was taken away and the new era fully began. That period of time is symbolic only in that it was also the amount of time that it took to purge Israel of the adults before they could enter into the Promised Land. At that time, it was a period of judgment, but the forty years from the resurrection to the destruction of the old temple was a time of mercy.

Remember how precise the measurements were for the altar in Moses' tabernacle (Lesson 4)? The new temple is no less precise. His measurements are also specific. He wandered and fasted in the desert for forty days. He finished the new creation on the sixth day and rested on the seventh. He rose or was rebuilt after three days, on the eighth day. These numbers should now be obvious to us. Jesus is the fulfillment of all the numbers, of all of God's Word.

Conclusion

Man's days are limited. "Behold, you have made my days a few handbreadths, and my lifetime is as nothing before you. Surely all mankind stands as a mere breath!" (Psalms 39:5). Yet God has joined Himself to us. He walked this earth less than forty years, was cut down like a flower in His prime, that we would be spared. Though our days fly by quickly, and though we deserve harsh judgment for our sins, God is merciful to us and has provided an ark in the Church to bring us safely to Himself in heaven. He has removed us from time and joined us to the eighth day in the waters of Holy Baptism. Soon all preparations will be over. He will complete the good work He has begun in us (Philippians 1:6).

Closing Prayer

O Lord, teach us to number our days and to remember that we belong to you, through Jesus Christ, our Lord. Amen.

Forty and Eight: A Generation of Mercy and the New Creation

The Generation Gap

What is a generation? How long is it? How old were your parents when you were born? Read **Numbers 32:13**.

Review the story of the flood by reading **Genesis 6–8**. Think about the numbers. How big was the ark? How long was the flood from start to finish? How long were they on the ark? How many people were on the ark? How many animals?

Noah's Saving Ark

While Noah and his family were in the dark, God sent rain for forty days and forty nights. Can you think of any other times that the Bible speaks of "forty days and forty nights"? Read **Matthew 4:1–2**; **1 Kings 19:7–8**; and **Deuteronomy 9:9**. Why fast for forty days and nights?

A New Sign for a New Covenant

Read **1 Peter 3:18–22**. What is the significance of the number eight?

Read **Genesis 17:11–12**. What day did circumcision take place? Read **Colossians 2:11–14**. What is the "circumcision made without hands"? Is there any significance to the number of the people on the ark to tie the ark to circumcision and therefore Baptism?

Forty Years to Prepare for the New Age

Read what Paul did long after his conversion and missionary journeys had begun in **Acts 21:26**. Now read **Acts 8:26–38**. How long were the temple sacrifices valid after Jesus rose from the dead? What does the Ethiopian eunuch teach us about the Word given to those who were waiting for the Messiah outside Palestine?

Read **Matthew 24:1–14**. What does Jesus say about the temple's future? How is what happened in 70 AD a testimony to the whole world? What is the temple that is torn down and rebuilt in three days?